CRISIS ON THE BORDER

CRISIS

ON THE

BORDER

An Eyewitness Account of Illegal Aliens, Violent Crime, and Cartels

MATT C. PINSKER
UNITED STATES FEDERAL SPECIAL PROSECUTOR

REGNERY
PUBLISHING
A Division of Salem Media Group

Regnery® is a registered trademark of Salem Communications Holding Corporation

ISBN 978-1-68451-010-8
ebook ISBN 978-1-68451-045-0

LCCN: 2019955225

Published in the United States by
Regnery Publishing
A Division of Salem Media Group
300 New Jersey Ave NW
Washington, DC 20001
www.Regnery.com

Manufactured in the United States of America

10 9 8 7 6 5 4 3 2 1

Books are available in quantity for promotional or premium use. For information on discounts and terms, please visit our website: www.Regnery.com.

To my wife,
for letting me go away for six months to the border

CONTENTS

AUTHOR'S NOTE

All opinions and views expressed in this book are mine; I am not speaking on behalf of the Department of Defense or the Department of Justice.

Throughout this book, I have omitted the names of fellow prosecutors, Border Patrol agents, U.S. Marshals, and many others I worked with. They do a tremendous job, but many of them are still engaged in fighting the cartels, and revealing their identities could put their lives at additional risk.

A CLEAR AND PRESENT DANGER

What I'm about to say might seem obvious, but I'm afraid to many members of Congress and to every governor of a sanctuary state or mayor of a sanctuary city it's a truth that needs to be told over and over again: a country that can't control its own borders is not a secure, sovereign nation.

The author of this book, an Army JAG officer who volunteered to help prosecute cases at the border, gives us an invaluable firsthand account of how Mexican drug cartels effectively control the Mexican side of the border, how a disproportionate number of those infiltrating the border have serious criminal records, and how illegal immigrants coming into the United States near Laredo came from as far away as Bangladesh.

Given how porous our southern border is, it should surprise no one that our enemies, including Islamist terrorists, see it as a tremendous vulnerability of which they can take advantage. Just as gangs, like MS-13, increase their number of foot soldiers through illegal immigration into this country, so do terrorist

1

cells; in fact, intelligence indicates there are terrorist training camps on the Mexican side of the border.

I have talked with U.S. Border Patrol agents who have told me that illegal immigration along our southern border isn't simply a matter of poor Mexicans or Central Americans seeking work, though of course there are plenty of those. But Border Patrol agents are also finding Korans, Muslim prayer books, prayer rugs, and terrorist training manuals brought by illegal immigrants who are categorized as OTMs (Other than Mexicans). Of course, not all Muslim immigrants are terrorists, but we know for certain that some come from terror-sponsoring countries and have terrorist connections.

In 2006, the Senate Committee on Homeland Security's Permanent Subcommittee on Investigations issued a report titled *Line in the Sand: Confronting the Threat at the Southwest Border*. That report had data that were alarming then and remain alarming today. The report noted that during 2005, the "Border Patrol apprehended approximately 1.2 million illegal aliens; of those 165,000 were from countries other than Mexico. Of the non-Mexican aliens, approximately 650 were from special interest countries. Special interest countries are those 'designated by the intelligence community as countries that could export individuals that could bring harm to our country in the way of terrorism.'"

The report continued: "The sheer increase of OTMs coming across the border makes it more difficult for Border Patrol agents to readily identify and process each, thereby increasing the chances that a potential terrorist could slip through the system. Moreover, there is no concrete mechanism for determining how many OTMs evade apprehensions and successfully enter the country illegally."

We know that Islamist terrorists are among these OTMs. Robert Mueller, who was then director of the FBI, testified, as noted in the report, that "there are individuals from countries with known al-Qa'ida connections who are changing their Islamic surnames to Hispanic-sounding names and obtaining false Hispanic identities, learning to speak Spanish and pretending to be Hispanic immigrants."

Indeed, there have been human-smuggling operations specializing in bringing Middle Eastern illegal immigrants into the United States via Mexico. The report stated plainly, "Members of Hezbollah, the Lebanon-based terrorist organization, have already entered the United States across our Southwest border. On March 1, 2005, Mahmoud Youssef Kourani [himself an illegal immigrant] pleaded guilty to providing material support to Hezbollah.... Kourani established residence among the Lebanese expatriate community in Dearborn, Michigan and began soliciting funds for Hezbollah terrorists back home in Lebanon. He is the brother of the Hezbollah chief of military operations in southern Lebanon."

After the 2015 Islamist terrorist attack in San Bernardino, California, I went out to help conduct a leadership training seminar for the San Bernardino County Sheriff's Department. At one point, I asked one of the deputies whether he was worried about there being more Islamist terrorist cells in San Bernardino. He told me, "General, we're worried there are cells like that all over the country." Indeed, the FBI is investigating possible terrorist cells nationwide. These cells are fed by illegal immigration—and as long as they find new recruits, they will not go away.

I spent more than thirty-six years as a soldier, including more than a dozen years with Delta Force and two years as its commander. I was involved in many high-profile missions abroad, including the 1980 Iran hostage rescue attempt, the 1992 hunt for Pablo Escobar in Colombia, and the Black Hawk Down incident in Mogadishu, Somalia. I have also served as the Deputy Under Secretary of Defense for Intelligence and worked for the CIA. But I can tell you this: While I have fought America's enemies abroad, the greatest danger we face right now isn't tanks on a battlefield in Europe or the Middle East. It isn't a nuclear war with Russia or China—though of course these remain active threats. It isn't even economic or cyber warfare, though these too are very serious threats. No—the greatest threat is if we do not assert our most basic right as a sovereign nation and control our borders. Without that, there will be no America to defend.

This book, *Crisis on the Border*, is a swift and compelling read. I urge you to read it—and to read the federal reports the author reproduces as appendices—and to let your congressman know you want America's borders enforced for the sake of our national security. To do anything less is irresponsible and a dereliction of political duty.

—Retired U.S. Army Lieutenant General William G. "Jerry" Boykin, former commander of Delta Force

CHAPTER 1

HOW AN ARMY LAWYER BECAME A FEDERAL SPECIAL PROSECUTOR

Our boat plowed through the choppy waters of the Rio Grande, a cold wind in our faces, a sense of dread beginning to build.

Our mission was grim.

A "floater" had been reported in the river east of Laredo, Texas. We were looking for a dead body, determined to do our duty as representatives of the Border Patrol by providing a proper burial.

What am I doing here? I wondered, looking at the two Border Patrol agents in the boat with me. They wore twenty pounds of body armor and tactical scarves over their faces. They carried military-style M4 rifles.

I was unarmed and wearing jeans, a button-down shirt, and a life jacket.

What am I doing here?

On the northern side of the river, the American side, we were completely isolated amid miles and miles of grazing land with no sign of Border Patrol and no backup.

On the southern side, the Mexican side, heavily armed twenty-somethings eyed us ominously. I was struck by their numbers; there were about a dozen of them, their faces covered in tattoos marking them as cartel members.

It occurred to me then that our floater's drowning had been no accident. The cartel's intense interest in our search made it clear that this nameless person had been murdered like many other ill-fated border crossers—probably for failing to pay the fees demanded by the cartels for safe passage.

We kept careful watch on the cartel members as we cruised past. It was unlikely they would open fire on us, but we couldn't rule out the possibility. Months earlier, they'd shot at a U.S. helicopter. And although cartel bosses were careful to avoid open warfare with the United States, their low-ranking foot soldiers— often drug addicts themselves—didn't necessarily think things through rationally.

What am I doing here? I wondered again.

■ ■ ■

My path to the Army's Judge Advocate General's (JAG) Corps was similar to the way many others entered military service—family tradition.

My dad had served as an Army doctor and transferred to the Army Reserve shortly before I was born. With the Reserve demanding just one weekend per month of my dad's time, the Army played very little role in my upbringing. The one big exception to this—which would leave a major impression on me—was the First Gulf War. Although the war was a quick, easy victory for the United States, many people forget that, at the time, Iraq had the fourth-largest military in the world, and we had been preparing for as many as fifty thousand casualties. Because of this, the Army mobilized my dad and many other medical professionals and sent them to Germany to be ready to treat the wounded.

I was three years old at the time. To explain my father's absence, my older brother told me, "You know how Superman and Batman beat up bad guys? There's a bad guy out there named Saddam Hussein, and daddy's helping beat him up."

To a three-year-old, hearing your dad compared to your favorite superheroes was pretty cool.

A decade and a half later, when I got to college, I had trouble adjusting to the rigorous academics of the College of William & Mary. After my first semester, I found myself on academic probation and at risk of being kicked out. I knew I had to make some major changes. The catalyst for change came during the second semester of my freshman year, when I decided to follow in my dad's footsteps toward military service and joined the Army Reserve Officers' Training Corp (ROTC).

Like many colleges, William & Mary had a strong military officer training program where, over the course of four years, students trained to serve as military leaders. This included physical training at six in the morning three times per week, plus classes and training activities for students to learn combat maneuvers and land navigation. ROTC added the structure to my life that I desperately needed. More importantly, it gave me a sense of purpose and belonging—a reason for my being there on campus. My grades improved, and I began participating in other extracurricular activities, including the varsity cheerleading squad, writing and producing a feature-length film, and even getting a resolution through the state legislature.

Of everything I did in college, nothing was more fulfilling and meaningful to me than the Army ROTC. This made my disqualification from the program during my junior year extremely difficult. At the time, I was taking medication for attention deficit disorder, which was prohibited. I will never forget the day my commanding officer, Lieutenant Colonel Monahan, broke the news to me. I kept a straight face in his office, but later, when I was alone, it was the only time during college that I cried.

But because of the discipline the ROTC had instilled in me, I was able to view it as a temporary setback and create a plan for finding an alternate route into the Army. I decided I would go to law schools at West Virginia University (J.D.) and George Washington University (LL.M.) and join the Army Reserve as an attorney and officer in the Judge Advocate General's Corps. As an Army Reservist, it was expected that I maintain civilian employment, so I first worked as a magistrate and then as a state prosecutor before switching to criminal defense. I eventually moved back to the town I grew up in, where I started my own criminal defense law firm and taught homeland security and criminal justice at Virginia Commonwealth University. Between running a law firm and teaching, I really enjoyed my civilian life. But it was my Army service that brought me to the border.

■ ■ ■

In fact, it was a single email that had led me away from my comfortable life as a criminal defense attorney and professor in my hometown of Richmond, Virginia.

The email claimed there was an "urgent need" for special prosecutors to prosecute immigration cases in federal courts along the southern border. This need stemmed from the Trump administration's "zero tolerance" crackdown on illegal immigration, which mandated that all who crossed the border illegally be prosecuted. This was a major change; illegal immigrants who flagrantly and openly violated our country's laws would no longer receive the ineffective and nonpunitive administrative procedures of the past, such as catch-and-release or simple deportation. Those methods had failed to deter illegal immigration in the past, allowed so many to slip into our country, overwhelmed our institutions, and made a mockery of our legal immigration system.

I stared at the email, nervous about what it would mean for me and my wife. But I felt called to serve. As an Army Reservist and member of the JAG Corps, it seemed perfectly tailored to my skills and experiences. And as a lifelong conservative, I felt a duty to take part in what I viewed as a long overdue change in U.S. policy.

In addition, with my wife and I in the advanced stages of family planning, I was yearning for one last adventure before children entered the picture.

I submitted my application and waited for a response.

A month later, I was informed that I had been selected as one of twenty-one judge advocates out of thousands from the Army, Navy, Air Force, Marine Corps, and Coast Guard.

Soon after, I received my orders calling me to active duty in just eleven days. Destination: Laredo, Texas, a border city of 260,000 people—95 percent Hispanic—that would be my home for the next six months.

■ ■ ■

As the sun began to set on the Rio Grande, the two Border Patrol agents in the boat with me determined that we had little chance of finding the dead body with nightfall approaching. We turned back, the cartel members still looking on from the river-bank and monitoring our every move.

For them, this was a small victory: another anonymous death, another murder for which there would be no justice.

Such murders are nearly a daily occurrence on the southern border, where a surging humanitarian crisis is playing out largely hidden from the public eye. But our politicians are unwilling to confront the crisis head-on, and our media are stymied when it comes to how to cover it.

For six months, I had an insider's view of this hidden crisis and played a small role in trying to bring order and justice to a border where lawlessness and chaos were rife. I saw firsthand the violence and the power of the organized crime bosses who dominate the border. I saw firsthand how lawlessness wins when our immigration policies aren't enforced.

And I prosecuted criminals who, in the past, would have been able to sneak into our country unimpeded.

That's what I was doing there.

CHAPTER 2

WELCOME TO LAREDO'S U.S. ATTORNEY'S OFFICE

When I arrived in Laredo, I was struck by the intense focus on security—layers upon layers of it, in fact—to protect us and our mission.

For starters, there was my personal security. During my initial briefing, I was told that I was absolutely forbidden from venturing into Mexico. This was disappointing; I had been looking forward to experiencing Mexico's food and culture. But as a U.S. government employee and prosecutor, I would be a desirable target for kidnapping, torture, and murder. This warning proved very real to me during my nights in downtown Laredo when I heard gunfire from the other side of the border as the Mexican Army fought the drug cartels or the cartels fought one another.

Some of the older federal prosecutors and public defenders spoke nostalgically of a time when they could leave the courthouse on lunch break, walk across the bridge over the Rio Grande to venture into Mexico for tacos, and walk back to work. This was before everything "went to shit," as they put it. Many hadn't crossed the border since the violence broke out in 2004.

Even on the American side of the border, I was instructed to keep a low profile. Laredo was a border town, and the cartels have a strong presence there with informants, enforcers, and foot soldiers. During our interactions with locals, we didn't disclose any work-related details. Instead, we gave locals vague cover stories about our jobs, saying we were "contractors" or "consultants."

There were also many layers of physical security at the building that was to be my office for the next six months.

Normally, the U.S. Attorney's Office would be attached to the local federal courthouse. In Laredo, though, the U.S. Attorney's Office is a fifteen-mile drive from the courthouse in an office park filled with warehouses. This was the closest location that could meet the strict security requirements of the Department of Justice—many of which I cannot discuss here except to say they go well beyond the security requirements of a normal office building.

As an Army Reservist, my first instinct upon arriving was to report to my new commander—in this case a civilian, the Assistant U.S. Attorney in Charge (AUSA-in-Charge). He was exceptionally friendly and personable and had practiced law for nearly thirty years. Over the next six months, he would teach me much about what it means to be a prosecutor and leader. Because of the political climate, almost every major decision involving a case had to be run through him. The AUSU-in-Charge had served for twelve years as an elected county attorney in Laredo and understood the city as well as anyone—and, like any good politician, he was extremely skilled at the schmoozing and small talk required to navigate the thorny issues that came across our desks constantly.

In addition to being exceptionally secured, the U.S. Attorney's Office in Laredo was very large, but felt oddly vacant. This was because it was grossly understaffed—hence the "urgent need" for special prosecutors like me. Given the number of cases the office prosecuted, there should have been fifteen line attorneys doing general prosecutions, plus several more in specialty roles handling cases involving organized crime and civil defense.

Instead, for most of my deployment, there were only five line prosecutors, including me and another JAG officer on this special assignment who had been a lieutenant and judge advocate in the Puerto Rico National Guard. Because of the crushing number of cases, the specialty attorneys were often diverted from dealing with organized crime and instead helped us handle ordinary illegal immigration prosecutions.

Staff retention at U.S. Attorney's Offices in border towns is a major problem. Federal prosecutor positions are highly coveted, so the new hires are almost all young, ambitious state prosecutors eager to get federal experience. Taking a position in an undesirable location like Laredo is how they get a foot in the door. They undertake the challenging work for a couple of years, and then, with that experience on their resumes, transfer to a more lucrative career in private practice or a different U.S. Attorney's Office in a much more desirable—and far less dangerous—location.

■ ■ ■

My first day in Laredo included a trip to the courthouse.

The AUSU-in-Charge assigned me to another attorney, who was nicknamed "Paco," who showed me the ropes. Paco would become a good friend. He had been on the job for only four months, but he was already knowledgeable about the quirks and personal preferences of each of the judges and knew which defense attorneys could be trusted in good-faith negotiations.

In blazing 120-degree heat, Paco and I arrived at the courthouse drenched in sweat, ready to handle the cases awaiting us.

The Kazen Courthouse, named for U.S. District Judge George Kazen, was originally planned to be one of the tallest buildings in Laredo. But it had been redesigned to just three stories after officials realized that people would be able to shoot at it from across the border in Mexico if it were any taller.

I followed Paco as he bypassed the security checkpoint through a side door with his keycard. Since I didn't have a keycard yet, several U.S. Marshals converged on me, nearly tackling me to the floor. Paco rescued me, explaining that I was with him and was new to the office.

Once they realized I was a federal prosecutor, the Marshals instantly changed their demeanor, warmly welcoming me to the team. For the next six months, I would feel a strong sense of camaraderie with them, many of whom had military backgrounds. I even met one Marshal who, in a previous job, had gone undercover as an illegal immigrant, sometimes letting himself be smuggled across the border and other times working to gain employment as an "illegal alien" with major U.S. corporations as part of an investigation into unlawful hiring practices. All of this was fascinating and helped prepare me for the range of experiences I might encounter in my new environment.

Paco took me into the courtroom, where we walked past the spectator benches and through the waist-high swinging gates to the "well" of the courtroom where the real work got done.

It was time to get started.

■ ■ ■

A typical day at the courthouse always began with reading—lots of reading.

Two Border Patrol agents would enter every morning, each wheeling a rolling suitcase full of "A-Files"—immigration files containing a defendant's biographical details, criminal record, biometrics, immigration history, and interview transcripts. We would read the "A-Files" of everyone being prosecuted that morning for misdemeanor illegal entry.

For anyone being charged with felony reentry, the Border Patrol agents would bring stacks of additional paperwork. But such cases were rare. For every fifty immigrants who could have been charged with felony reentry, we typically prosecuted only one because we lacked the manpower for felony investigations and prosecutions. Even with a guilty plea, it takes a hundred times more work to get a felony conviction in federal court than a misdemeanor conviction, and we just didn't have the time or resources to do that.

Police officers and Border Patrol agents liked to show up in court for their cases that involved something more serious than illegal entry—such as human smuggling, gun running, drugs, or child pornography.

When law enforcement officers were present, I would ask if there was anything unusual about an upcoming case that I should know. In one instance, a defendant had been holding illegal aliens hostage at gunpoint at a safe house until they paid the smugglers their "release fee." (Human smugglers like to spring unexpected costs and fees onto the persons they were paid to traffic into the country.) Normally, such a violent act would be the basis to deny a bond. But in speaking with a police officer involved with the case, I learned that the defendant was cooperating with investigators and providing useful information, and if I gave him bond, he would be able to bring down the other smugglers. Based on that, I agreed to the deal. In another case, the court's Pretrial Services recommended a bond for a human trafficker who didn't have any criminal record, but I had him held without bond after speaking with the arresting officer, who told me how the guy had been exploiting children.

■ ■ ■

On a typical day, we would handle between one hundred and two hundred cases involving illegal entry. Work would begin soon after nine in the morning when the judge entered the courtroom, and a clerk would announce that court was in session.

After the law clerk called the court to order, the judge would take his seat and we would begin the docket. In a line in the front were the defendants being "initialed," which meant that they were making their first court appearance after being charged with a crime. Most of these crimes involved smuggling drugs and firearms, human trafficking, and the few cases of felony reentry we might prosecute.

Some of the defendants wore orange jumpsuits. Others were in the same clothes they had been arrested in. All of them had chains around their ankles and wrists. More than 90 percent of them were men.

The judge would first address them as a group, explaining that this was their initial appearance—which meant that the judge would review their charges, determine who their lawyer would be, and decide whether they should be offered bond while their cases were pending.

Most of the cases I dealt with were heard by Judge Song (whose full name is Diana Song Quiroga). She was kind, friendly, and professional. After speaking to the defendants as a group, she would address each one individually. The defendants who did not speak English wore headphones through which they heard the voice of an interpreter.

Judge Song read the charges against each defendant and a synopsis of the facts. She asked if they understood the charges. Most said "yes." Others nodded. But a few said "no" and protested their innocence. Occasionally, defendants would claim not to understand the charge, almost invariably because they wanted to be difficult. When that happened, Judge Song would maintain a poker face and patiently explain the charge to the defendant again as if she were talking to a child.

Judge Song then reviewed whether the defendants had legal counsel. Occasionally, a defendant had retained private counsel, but most of the time the defendant would request a court-appointed lawyer, which usually meant the appointment of someone from the Office of the Federal Public Defender. The public defenders I worked with in Laredo were exceptionally skilled in criminal defense and were dedicated to their clients. The defendants were lucky to have them as their attorneys.

Most of those being charged in federal court already had lengthy criminal records and had previously been represented by federal public defenders. Quite often, they would ask Judge Song to reappoint the lawyer who had previously represented them. If the lawyer was available, the judge would oblige. And on those rare occasions when defendants were upset with their assigned lawyers (usually because they blamed them for losing a previous case), Judge Song would appoint them a new lawyer.

Finally, the judge decided whether the defendant would be held without bond. Bond decisions are based on whether a defendant is a danger to the community or a potential flight risk. Many defendants were Mexican citizens or U.S. citizens with very close ties to Mexico, and because the courthouse was only a short sprint from the border, most defendants were held without bond.

I usually agreed when bond was granted, but not always—especially when I suspected that a defendant was tied to organized crime. If I did object to bond for any reason at an initial appearance, the defendant would remain in custody and a proper bond hearing would be scheduled for five days later. One case involved a human trafficker who had used his vehicle as a weapon and tried to ram the arresting officer's vehicle. Pretrial Services recommended bond for this client. I objected and bond was denied, at least initially. But another prosecutor handled the bond hearing five days later and agreed to a bond.

In rare instances, the opposite happened and I would support a bond when the pretrial staff had recommended "no bond." In one such a case, I knew from the arresting officer that the defendant was cooperating with law enforcement and providing useful information—and might even be willing to go undercover wearing a wire. I had a private, off-the-record conference with the defense attorney and the judge; back in court, the judge issued a reasonable bond without having to say anything about why. Defense attorneys were always grateful when their clients received a bond because it got their client out of jail, which might give them an opportunity to do things which would deduct points from the sentencing guidelines.

Material Witnesses

After initial appearances (which we called "initials"), the next group to come before the judge included detained material witnesses. These were illegal aliens who had been caught trying to enter the country but were not being charged with a crime. Instead, we were prosecuting the person smuggling them into the United States—usually the foot guide leading them through the desert or the driver of a vehicle bringing them in.

Because of their illegal status, we knew they would likely disappear if we released them from U.S. custody. If we deported them, we had no means to get them to court later. The only solution was to hold them in detention for the duration of the criminal proceedings of the person who was charged.

Obviously, this was tough on the material witnesses. Most illegal aliens were simply convicted and quickly deported, often within seventy-two hours of being caught, but material witnesses could be held for three to six months—and sometimes longer. They understandably weren't happy with their status, but almost all of them were cooperative. Still, every so often we would have someone who would be difficult. One day in court, a material witness simply refused to wear translator headphones. When he finally did put them on, he angrily told Judge Song that he would not cooperate. He wanted to plead guilty to illegal entry and go home. We should pick one of the other fifty-five illegals caught in the truck with him to be our witness, he said.

Judge Song was beyond kind and understanding with this defendant. She gently repeated that this was how the American legal system worked and that defense attorneys and prosecutors can force a witness to come to court. Moreover, an uncooperative material witness could be charged with contempt, which would lengthen his time in detention. Judge Song didn't state that last part as a threat, but as friendly advice. And it worked!

Sometimes we had other issues with material witnesses. One case involved two illegals being smuggled in a Honda Civic. When the driver approached an immigration checkpoint on the highway, he panicked and sped off, zipping recklessly—over one hundred miles per hour—between other motorists and terrifying the two illegal aliens who begged him to slow down and let them out. The driver complied, then did a 180-degree turn as he illegally crossed onto the other side of the highway and tried to escape in the opposite direction, only to speed into a police-laid tire puncture trap.

One of the illegal aliens was never found—he either died in the desert or disappeared in the United States. The other, a self-identified eighteen-year-old Guatemalan, was arrested that same day. When he learned he would be held as a material witness to testify against the driver, he changed his story and said he was only seventeen years old. With the assistance of the Guatemalan Embassy, I verified that he was, in fact, seventeen. Because he was a juvenile, we could not hold him as a material witness and instead had to release him for immediate deportation.

Without our witness, we could no longer prosecute the driver for human trafficking. Instead, we prosecuted him for fleeing from a checkpoint. It was still a felony, but under new sentencing guidelines, he received only probation and no jail time, which meant that he was soon back on the streets—and possibly back in business as a human smuggler.

CHAPTER 3

MASS GUILTY PLEAS

After initial court appearances, bond hearings, and preliminary exams (where we show the court that we have sufficient evidence to detain the defendant until trial) came the mass guilty pleas of illegal aliens—the main event of the day.

Half of the illegal immigrants received a generous plea deal: "time served." Whatever time they had spent in detention—usually measured in hours, not days—counted as their jail sentences, and they were deported, many of them to Mexico, where they were free to begin their illegal journeys to the United States all over again. That's not speculation; it's a fact. I often saw the same defendants wearing the same clothes back in court just a few days after they had been convicted and deported, which was obviously frustrating to us and could make our jobs seem pointless. Over the course of my six months in Laredo, I prosecuted (and got convictions for) many people multiple times, some as many as three or four different times.

But the reason I and other prosecutors offered generous plea deals wasn't because we were charitable; it was because we lacked the resources to detain everyone while pending trial and lacked the prosecutors and judges to take all these cases to trial. The U.S. Attorney's Office in Laredo is swamped with hundreds of border-related cases every day, and if just 1 percent of the persons charged with illegal entry went to trial instead of taking a plea deal, the entire court system would grind to a halt. In fact, if the public defenders had teamed up and demanded trials for all their clients, most pending cases would likely have been dismissed because we couldn't meet the defendants' constitutional right to a speedy trial. In order to expedite prosecutions, we offered misdemeanor plea deals to illegal immigrants who had been deported multiple times—even if they had past felony drug convictions or were registered sex offenders. Nowhere else but at a border prosecutor's office would such serious criminals be treated so generously.

I didn't feel good about this, but there was little I could do to stop it; it's the way of life in Laredo and other border towns where the court systems are completely overwhelmed trying to process hundreds of illegal immigrants every day. Although the job of a prosecutor is to fight for justice, with the overwhelming numbers we were facing and complete lack of resources and support, we were just trying to stay afloat.

Typically, we processed between 75 and 150 guilty pleas—and sometimes more than 200—every day, with the trend moving steadily upward during my six months there. About 90 percent of them were from young men, usually in their twenties and thirties, who were looking for work.

To free up his regular prosecutors to handle crimes other than illegal immigration, the AUSA-in-Charge had me and a lieutenant do most of the illegal immigration cases for most of our deployment. We started out by alternating which weeks we'd be in court. But in the six months we were in Laredo, the volume of illegal immigration cases increased so much that we were soon both at the courthouse at the same time, running our own dockets in separate courtrooms.

In court at the start of each morning, an army of public defenders would show up to speak individually with the defendants (all of the public defenders were bilingual), and then all but one would leave. The remaining lawyer would handle the court proceedings using notes left by the other public defenders.

For security and fire code reasons, we could only have approximately forty defendants in the courtroom at a time, and processing each group took between thirty and sixty minutes, depending on which judge was running the docket. This meant that in a day with two hundred defendants, it could take up to five hours to process everyone.

Inside each illegal alien's "A-File" was a mugshot, fingerprints and other biometric records, a narrative of the circumstances leading to the person's arrest, a transcript of an interview with the defendant, and the defendant's immigration history and criminal record. Because many illegal immigrants were repeat offenders, it was easy to dig up their records. If a defendant had not previously lived in the United States, it was more difficult because they often gave false names, provided false ages (we don't prosecute juveniles), and some aliens from Central America would lie and say they were from Mexico, hoping to be deported there so they could hop across the border again.

In one case, a defendant's A-File tagged him as Guatemalan, but he insisted to his federal public defender that he was Mexican.

His lawyer asked us to correct the record. When I checked the file, I saw that in 2011 the defendant had been arrested for illegal entry and deported to Guatemala. I pointed this out to the public defender. "Maybe he's moved?" I politely suggested.

The lawyer borrowed a couple documents from the file and conferred with his client. Minutes later, he returned with a sheepish grin and said, "My guy just remembered. He's from Guatemala after all." We saw stunts like this all the time.

■ ■ ■

Every morning prior to appearing in court, the public defenders briefed the illegal aliens in the courthouse detention area about their legal rights, options, and the process of the day. Then they met for a few minutes individually with their clients to go over specifics.

In my opinion, the public defenders had the toughest jobs and the toughest working conditions of anyone in the courthouse. The detention area in the back consisted of two cells that were about twenty-five feet by twenty-five feet. It was enough space for forty people, but they rarely held that few. The crowded cells were poorly ventilated, and the temperature was often above ninety degrees. By the time they got to the courtroom, the defendants and their lawyers would be dripping with sweat.

As bad as the heat was, it was the odor that made things miserable. Unsurprisingly, deodorant and hygiene are not priorities for illegal immigrants during their harrowing journeys to the United States. Those journeys often meant swimming through the contaminated Rio Grande or wearing the same clothes for days in the desert. Making matters worse, the short-term detention facility had no showers or laundry facilities, so illegal immigrants were brought to court in the same clothes they were arrested in, and possibly had been wearing and sweating in for weeks. With everyone in a hot, crowded, and confined space, you can imagine how terrible the odor was. There was one security guard who wore Vicks VapoRub under her nose to keep the stench away.

Despite the adverse working conditions, the federal public defenders did their jobs with utmost professionalism. Part of that job was asking defendants if they wanted their nation's consulate notified of the charges against them, which is their right under international law. The idea is that if you are caught up in the criminal justice system of a foreign country, your own country might want to look out for your welfare and ensure that your rights are not being violated.

Most Mexicans did not want to notify their consulate, but about half of the Guatemalans, Hondurans, and Salvadorans did. To me, this seemed ironic, because immigrants from these countries were the ones most likely to be seeking asylum. I could not understand why they would want to notify the very government from which they claimed to be fleeing, and this made me extremely skeptical of their requests for asylum. Regardless, the public defenders would make a list and give it to me and the other prosecutors so the U.S. government could fulfill its international obligation and notify the aliens' respective consulates.

In meeting with their clients, the federal public defenders would explain the pros and cons of asking for trial or entering a guilty plea. Of the thousands of aliens processed while I was in Laredo, only a single defendant had a trial, with everyone else taking the generous plea deals we offered.

■ ■ ■

Before appearing in court for their mass guilty pleas, the illegal immigrants would be divided almost equally into two groups.

The Group 1 included aliens who had no criminal or immigration history in the United States. While some had previously resided here, none had ever been deported. Instead, they had voluntarily left the country at some point and were now trying to enter illegally. Members of Group 1 were offered a standard plea deal: For admitting their guilt, they were sentenced to "time served" and deportation, which would sometimes occur that very day if the person was Mexican. At the longest, it would occur within a week. If these defendants demanded a trial—which they never did—they would have had to wait in detention for 30–60 days. Because the evidence of guilt was overwhelming, it was inevitable that they would be found guilty anyway. The plea deal was an easy choice.

But Group 2 was a bit different. Those members also were charged with misdemeanor illegal entry, but nearly everyone in Group 2 also had a criminal record and had been deported before. This meant that, in theory, we could have charged them with a felony for illegal reentry into the United States. Instead of a misdemeanor charge that came with a maximum six-month sentence, a felony conviction could mean years in prison. But we also offered these defendants a generous plea deal: For admitting their guilt, their charges were downgraded from felonies to misdemeanors. Another easy choice.

■ ■ ■

Each week, there would be a few defendants who balked, at least initially, at the prospect of pleading guilty. This usually was because they were confused about the American legal system and did not understand that the federal magistrate court was a criminal court—not an immigration court that could hear their asylum requests. When this happened, the public defenders would ask us to delay the defendants' court appearances for a week so their clients could consult an immigration attorney. I never objected to this. I recognized just how scary and confusing the judicial system is even to Americans, let alone aliens who don't speak the language. I didn't begrudge anyone doing their due diligence before entering a guilty plea. In every instance that I encountered, the defendants entered guilty pleas a few days later.

Many other times, individuals were medically unfit to enter guilty pleas. I often had a public defender whisper to me that a certain illegal alien was suffering from heroin or alcohol withdrawal and because of that was incapable of understanding the proceedings. Sometimes we'd even have to rush them to the hospital before their withdrawal symptoms killed them. It was alarming just how many illegal aliens caught entering the United States were addicted to drugs. I would always agree to reset those cases and keep the plea offers open.

■ ■ ■

Not all illegal aliens were offered generous plea deals.

In 99 percent of the cases, the Border Patrol used a points system to decide which cases to prosecute as felonies. After an alien was arrested for illegally entering the country, a Border Patrol agent would review the alien's criminal and immigration history and assign points to it. For example, if the person had a prior 1325 (which is shorthand for misdemeanor illegal entry), the person would get two points. If the person had committed a more serious crime and had previously served more than two years in prison, the person would be assessed six points. At a certain threshold—which I am purposely not disclosing—instead of a misdemeanor illegal entry under section 1325 of U.S. criminal law, the charge instead would be a felony of illegal reentry under section 1326. In court, we had a shorthand where we would simply refer to cases as either a "1325" or a "1326."

There were some cases where defendants met the points threshold for a felony but were still charged with misdemeanors. This would happen when, under federal sentencing guidelines, a defendant—even if convicted of a felony—would likely get no more than six months in federal prison. From our perspective, it made little sense to spend the extra time pursuing a felony conviction when the sentence would be the same as for a misdemeanor.

Other times, we had cases where a person did not meet the points threshold for a felony but was charged with a felony anyway. This happened most often in cases involving illegal aliens who had previously pleaded guilty to extremely serious crimes but had received little to no jail time (and therefore not enough points by our usual standards to pursue a felony case). These cases often involved child molesters who had been sentenced to very little jail time—despite having previously been convicted of extremely heinous acts. The reason why prosecutors and judges had previously imposed lenient sentences was because they knew that the conviction itself would get the person deported, and it made little sense to spend U.S. tax dollars incarcerating someone who would simply be kicked out of the country after serving his sentence. While this does make financial sense, this also frequently means that an illegal alien who had been convicted for molesting children would receive a more lenient sentence than a U.S. citizen who had done the same thing. Now, after serving their brief sentences and being deported, they had tried to illegally reenter the United States and had been caught. They had caught a break the first time by getting a sweetheart deal from state prosecutors, but we'd nail them this time.

■ ■ ■

After the public defenders finished screening their clients and the necessary corrections, changes, or dismissals were made, we brought the defendants before the judge. The defendants would be marched from the detention area in the courthouse and into the well of the courtroom forty at a time.

During my time in Laredo, there were three rotating judges: Judge Song, Judge John Kazen—son of George Kazen, for whom the courthouse was named—and Judge Sam Sheldon.

Members of Group 1 were usually unrestrained, but those in Group 2 wore ankle and wrist cuffs connected to a chain around their waists. Unlike the overheated detention area, the courtroom was heavily air conditioned, and many of the illegal aliens were visibly cold; some were even shivering. They wore the same clothes they had tried crossing the desert in, which usually consisted of a t-shirt and jeans or shorts. Many also wore sandals.

They were lined up before the judge, usually in three rows of ten to fifteen people. The federal public defender announced the changes we had agreed on—such as correcting records, dismissing cases involving juveniles or where the statute of limitations applied, or resetting the "status date" one week out for any defendants demanding a trial—and fully expected that they would change their minds.

Once those preliminary administrative matters were out of the way, we would begin the process of accepting guilty pleas. I say process, because unlike state misdemeanor courts, we couldn't simply accept a guilty plea and move on. Instead, the judges made a lengthy effort to establish on the record that each person's plea was being done knowingly and voluntarily. This process would take Judge Song anywhere from thirty to seventy-five minutes per each forty-person group, depending on how cooperative everyone was. Judge Sheldon could do it in about thirty minutes, but it almost always took Judge Kazen more than an hour. Regardless, the process and procedure were the same each day.

Judge Song would verify the defendants' names and ask them a litany of questions, including: were they under the influence of drugs or medications; had they ever suffered a brain injury; did they understand the charges against them and the possible penalties; did they realize that they could be deported and forfeit any right to become a citizen; had they consulted with a lawyer; were they fully aware of their legal rights (some of which the judge enumerated); could they confirm that they were making a guilty plea with full knowledge of what they were doing and of their own free will; would their defense attorneys attest to that; and so on.

In response to each question, we would go down the line, getting a "si" or "no" from each illegal alien. After the last person in the group had given a "yes" or "no" answer, the judge would move on to the next question, and the whole process would repeat itself.

After the questioning was complete, a Border Patrol agent read a scripted paragraph stating that each defendant was an alien who was in the country illegally. The judge asked the defendants how they wanted to plead. After they pleaded guilty, the judge confirmed that the plea had been made knowingly, voluntarily, and truthfully. The judge warned that repeat offenses would be punished more severely, pronounced the sentence, and asked if the defendants had any final questions.

As simple as this process sounds, it wasn't simple at all. Some aliens would not or could not give straight answers, and some seemed incapable of understanding what was going on. (A public defender once commented to me, "It doesn't take much intelligence to cross the border, but it does take some intelligence to understand a guilty plea.") Mexican nationals almost never had problems going through this process, so U.S. Marshals, at the request of federal public defenders, made a point of putting a Mexican defendant first in line to set a good example for everyone else. The idea was that even if subsequent people in line didn't really understand, they could simply emulate and copy what the person in front of them had just said and done.

Still, it was a frustrating and slow process for everyone. Many times, aliens refused to answer the judge's preliminary questions and just tried to plead guilty, even shouting, "I'm guilty and want to go home!" When this happened, Judge Song would kindly reply, "I hear you and understand what you are saying. However, we have to go through this process. It is important that we establish that your guilty plea is voluntary." She might have to repeat that phrase multiple times, and eventually the alien would give up and resume answering her questions.

Within a few days of being deported, many members of Group 1 would be back in court as members of Group 2 after having been caught—again—crossing the border illegally. And the processing of Group 2 took much longer because the judge had to review the criminal record and immigration history of each defendant. For most past criminal convictions like assault, drug dealing, and DUI, the judge would read those out loud and explain why the alien was receiving the sentence he got. However, if a conviction was for something such as rape, sexual assault, or child molestation, the judge wouldn't say that out loud because the other illegal aliens might take offense and try to kill the convicted rapist or molester. Instead, the judge would use a euphemism, such as "an interesting conviction back in 2017" or "serious criminal history."

Defendants were permitted to make a statement before sentencing, though few said anything. However, some told the judge about how bad things were in their country of origin or about family members they had in the United States. It was here where I heard many heart-wrenching tales of how horrible conditions were at home for many of them—the brutal conditions they had endured in trying to illegally enter the United States, how they had been preyed upon and exploited by coyotes and cartels, as well as how many of them were separated from family members (often their children) here in the United States. These were powerful stories, but they didn't excuse the unlawful conduct of entering the country illegally.

One time, instead of telling a tale of personal tragedy and hardship, one woman simply said, "Thank you to all services who took care of us. I apologize. Thank you." Her statement caused me to look up from my papers, stunned. Others did, as well. The statement was repeated, word for word, by the next defendant in line.

It reminded me that many of these defendants came from countries where law enforcement officials could be as corrupt and dangerous as criminals, engaging in robbery, rape, and beatings. In contrast, our Border Patrol agents rescued many of these illegal aliens from the harsh desert, where they might have died (some certainly did). The Border Patrol agents provided food, medical attention, and shelter. They behaved, as I saw, with the utmost professionalism. They are the true heroes of the border— and their greatest enemies, I soon discovered, were the drug cartels.

CHAPTER 4

HOW ORGANIZED CRIME CONTROLS THE BORDER

Nearly every illegal alien I prosecuted in Laredo had been smuggled into the United States with the assistance of the Mexican drug cartels. From reading the A-Files, it looked as if 99 percent of all people illegally crossing the border were going through the cartels, rather than just trying to get across themselves. The reason the illegal aliens are paying the cartels between six thousand and eight thousand dollars to be smuggled into the United States instead of just crossing on their own accord is because the cartels have physically seized control of the border and divided it into their own territories. The cartels have militarized their sections of the border and carefully monitor and control them. If they catch people in their territory trying to cross illegally without paying smuggling fees, the cartels will murder them and dump their bodies in the Rio Grande. The reason they are so brutal to illegal aliens is because the business of illegal immigration is worth approximately between fifteen and twenty-five billion dollars per year (more than the NFL,

MLB, and NBA combined). So if aliens could illegally enter the United States for free, the cartels would be out a lot of money. This creates an ironic situation where the number one force securing the United States–Mexican border against illegal immigration isn't the Border Patrol, but the Mexican drug cartels! The power vacuum the U.S. government has created by failing to secure the border has enabled this situation to develop.

Reading the interview transcripts of arrested illegal aliens, I often marveled at the sophisticated system of safe houses used to get immigrants from South and Central America through Mexico. Along this harrowing journey, illegal aliens are often abused, starved, and beaten by the coyotes who smuggle them to the cartels' territory along the Rio Grande.

Many of the same networks and resources—boats, disposable cell phones, false documents, foot guides, drivers, and money for bribes—used in smuggling drugs can smuggle people, and the drug cartels have diversified criminal portfolios that include not just drug smuggling and human trafficking, but also gun smuggling, racketeering, and kidnapping. In court, we frequently saw defendants with horrible disfigurations, including burns, scars, and amputations—the result of being tortured by the cartels who had kidnapped them and held them for ransom.

In Nuevo Laredo, which is on the Mexican side of the Rio Grande, cartel-affiliated gangs lurked at places like the Nuevo Laredo bus station and looked for recently deported Mexicans to kidnap, abducting them at gunpoint. The victims were tortured into divulging the contact information of family members from whom the cartels could extort payment for the unsolicited "service" of "helping" their relatives reenter the United States, regardless of whether the aliens wanted to or not. Once the cartels had their unwilling human cargo in safe houses on the American side of the border, the victims' families would be contacted for further payment.

My first experience of a case like this involved an illegal alien who had been deported after a third DUI and a conviction in state court of "indecent contact with a child." He was caught reentering the country just three days later. Because we charged him with a felony, he had a stronger incentive than most defendants to fight his charges. At his preliminary hearing, he looked very indignant while seated at the defense table in handcuffs and an orange jumpsuit.

In a preliminary hearing, we only had to show probable cause that the defendant had committed the crime for which he had been charged. But in his closing remarks, the public defender surprised me by saying, "Your Honor, I do want to go on the record to mention the Brady obligation of the government, and that the government is required to turn over exculpatory evidence."

Any time a defense attorney mentions "Brady," it's a big deal, especially in a formal hearing like this. As a matter of law, prosecutors are required to turn over any "exculpatory evidence," which means evidence that might indicate innocence. It's a serious ethics violation if prosecutors fail to do this, and prosecutors have gone to prison for failing to comply. Out of an abundance of caution, I would always disclose all evidence to the defense counsel so that everything I had, they had. Still, when this attorney mentioned Brady, I grabbed the defendant's A-File and starting rifling through it, worried that I had missed something. But I hadn't.

During the bond hearing, the defense attorney advised the court that his defendant, mere hours after being deported from the United States after serving a lengthy prison sentence, had gone to a bus station, where he had been kidnapped. His kidnappers drove him to the border and ordered him at gunpoint to cross the Rio Grande back into the United States. Fearing for his life, the defendant had done as he was told, and a couple days after getting to the American side of the river, he was caught and arrested by the Border Patrol.

The public defender said that if we had any evidence that might support his client's story, we needed to turn it over. As far as I knew, we had none. The alien either had never said this to the Border Patrol or he had, but the Border Patrol had failed to document it. I was both alarmed and bewildered by this story. But if the defendant's story was true, I had a moral and legal duty to dismiss the felony charge and merely ask that the defendant be deported once again.

The judge ordered that, for now, the defendant continue to be held without bond. I asked the public defender if he believed his client's story. He shrugged and said, "It's possible. It's known to happen. And we're hearing similar stories more often." I asked other lawyers and Border Patrol agents, and they told me that it is a regular practice in Mexico for the cartels to actively seek out recently deported aliens, kidnap them, and force them at gunpoint to reenter the United States. However, we also had to contend with the fact that illegal aliens sometimes falsely make this claim, trying to play the system to get a lighter sentence.

I soon had many cases that involved similar stories, none of which could be proven or disproven, including another defendant who had been arrested only a few days after being deported. He claimed that after his deportation, he had gone to the Nuevo Laredo bus station, where he was approached by people who were either law enforcement officials or cartel members disguised as law enforcement officials. They demanded seven thousand dollars to help him back across the border. The man said he refused and told them that he only had three thousand dollars, hoping that some money would placate them and that they would spare his life. After taking his money, they contacted his family in Mexico and told them that they had been hired to get him across the border. Then they forced him across.

Judge Kazen asked the defendant if his lawyer knew all this. The defendant said his lawyer advised him that if he pleaded guilty, he would face thirty days in prison; if he went to trial, it would take much longer, and all he cared about was getting home. Judge Kazen, perhaps out of sympathy, sentenced him to just fifteen days in prison.

Sometimes the cartels kidnapped illegal aliens and used them for their drug trafficking operations. In one case, we had an illegal alien deported after he had been convicted and served time for drug distribution. He was arrested again days later and charged with illegal reentry. He told the court that just two hours after he was deported, drug cartel members abducted him at the Nuevo Laredo bus station. The cartel members tortured and beat him. They wanted to extort money from his family, but because of his time in prison in the United States, he had lost contact with them. The cartel members drove him to the Rio Grande, put drugs on him (he didn't say what kind), and ordered him to cross the river into the United States. The cartel members explained that in exchange for "helping" him across the border, he was going to carry a drug shipment. He said that they stabbed him in the stomach after he initially refused. In court, he lifted his shirt to show the stab wound.

In addition to the cartels, there are human smuggling organizations (HSOs) that operate independently or sometimes in coordination with the cartels, paying them for "protection" while in their territory. When there's money to be made, even criminals can be very cooperative. The most successful HSOs were small, family-run operations that moved too few people to attract much attention from U.S. law enforcement. As prosecutors, we had a strong desire to bring down HSOs. But as soon as one went down, another would take its place.

On average, an HSO or cartel will charge between six thousand and eight thousand dollars to smuggle someone into the United States, with half of it paid up front and the other half due shortly after crossing the border. But the cartels are very flexible in their prices (whatever they can get away with) and how they structure payments (sometimes with hefty interest). I saw illegals who had paid as little as five hundred dollars for passage and others who paid as much as twenty-eight thousand dollars.

Some human smuggling agreements are written out as formal contracts, as I learned not at the border, but in Virginia. An attorney friend of mine represented a woman who had received a "demand letter" from a lawyer representing a "coyote" (a trafficker of illegal aliens). The woman, a legal immigrant, had signed a contract with the coyote to smuggle her son into the United States. The coyote accused her of failing to pay the balance of the smuggling fee, and his lawyer threatened to sue her to collect the remainder plus interest.

When I first saw the letter, I was flabbergasted by its absurdity and figured the coyote must have forged or stolen the letterhead of the law firm which had sent it. I did not think a real lawyer would be stupid enough to send this letter; even a first-year law student knows a contract for an illegal service is not valid and is completely unenforceable. But it turned out that it was from a real lawyer. My friend, however, who represented the woman pro bono, convinced the coyote's moronic lawyer to withdraw the demand letter.

Illegal aliens apprehended near the border rarely have more than twenty dollars in cash on them. They are coming from countries like Guatemala and Honduras, where the average annual income is between two thousand and three thousand dollars per year, and they were typically making far less than that. They're broke and can't afford the smuggling fees themselves, so the ones actually paying the cartels to smuggle them into the United States are family members already in the United States (both legally and illegally). These family members, in cumulatively transferring between fifteen billion and twenty-five billion dollars to the cartels each year, perpetuate the cartels' operations of murder, destruction, and human misery (as, of course, do American drug users). Although these family members enrich the cartels and fuel the crisis at the border, they are almost never prosecuted. Not going after the money source may be the greatest failing of the U.S. government in its efforts to secure the border. In fact, in the entirety of my time on the border, I heard of only one such prosecution—and it only happened by accident as part of a much larger investigation into an HSO. It was a very sad case where a Deferred Action for Childhood Arrivals (DACA) recipient had gone into a Walmart to help her boyfriend wire money to a cartel to smuggle one of his family members into the United States. She was charged with a felony, lost her DACA status, and would likely be deported.

The cartels recognize that every person they bring across the border is a possible future referral for more business, because once this illegal alien is successfully in the United States, he will want to pay for his relatives to also be smuggled into the United States. And once those relatives are in the United States, they will do the same for their relatives too. It's "chain immigration" by illegal means. Many people want to come to the United States, and in the absence of effective enforcement of our immigration laws, the cartels determine who does.

■ ■ ■

Whether moving drugs or people across the border, the cartels' revenue depends on controlling territory, and they do not hesitate to use deadly force to protect it. Out on the river in a Border Patrol boat, I could see firsthand how well the cartels secured their territory. Fishermen relaxed in chairs approximately every mile along the river on both the U.S. and Mexican sides. These, however, weren't real fishermen. This stretch of the Rio Grande was contaminated because of a broken sewage pipe nearby. No sane person would fish here. The river stank, the water was a putrid green filled with garbage and debris, and the Border Patrol agents told me they had recently seen the cartel members dump a body into the river. These "fishermen" were lookouts for the cartels. They tracked and reported the Border Patrol's movements and made sure that no one crossed the border without the cartels' permission. Even though we knew they were lookouts, there is nothing inherently illegal about sitting in a chair along the Rio Grande in the 115-degree heat. The lookouts knew we couldn't touch them, especially on the Mexican side.

As far as jobs in organized crime go, theirs was a low-risk job and one of the best. In my entire time on the border, we never arrested a single fisherman-lookout. (In fact, we smiled and waved as we went past in our patrol boat, and they waved back.) And it was well paid. In Mexico, the minimum wage is between

$5.10 and $8.80 per day, and these "fishermen" were being paid fifty dollars per day.

■ ■ ■

In addition to the lookouts, there would be armed enforcers in the areas of the Rio Grande most conducive to illegal entry. While the lookouts were usually just poor Mexicans being paid by the cartels, these enforcers more often were actual cartel members. Even from a distance, we could sometimes see the tattoos covering their faces. We could also see the bulges in their waistlines indicating semi-concealed firearms. In Mexico, where private gun ownership is illegal, these gangsters are the only ones with guns, which is a large reason why they hold so much of the country hostage.

The Rio Grande, despite its tame appearance, is an extremely dangerous river to cross. Its water levels rise and fall quickly and with little warning. If you are weighed down by luggage and are a poor swimmer to begin with (and that describes most illegal immigrants), the unpredictable river can be fatal. In addition, the "coyotes" sometimes deliberately drown people in the river. Why would they drown their own customers? I asked that very question of a public defender, and he told me the coyotes had no qualms about killing someone who was slowing down the group and putting them at risk of capture. Nor did they hesitate to drown someone who refused to pay his full fare across the river. They did that as a warning to others.

Deaths happen often enough in the Rio Grande through intentional or unintentional drowning that one of the Border Patrol's duties is to look for "floaters" in the river.

■ ■ ■

I tagged along on missions with the Border Patrol whenever I could, and what I witnessed was more troubling than I could have imagined. One thing I learned early on was that we really do need a border wall—at least in areas like Laredo that are densely populated and have roads, infrastructure, and neighborhoods.

Laredo Community College, for instance, constructed an eight-foot-tall security fence on its southern edge just 150 yards from the Rio Grande. After doing so, the number of complaints they had about illegal immigrants trespassing on the campus dropped from multiple times per week to nearly zero.

Do I believe this eight-foot fence stopped any illegal aliens from entering this country? No. But it did reroute some aliens to other sections of the border. A border wall that did this on a much larger scale would make the Border Patrol's job much easier, because the Border Patrol could then concentrate its forces at certain choke points. This was exactly what they did with the fence around the community college. Other times, the school's fence would slow down illegal aliens trying to get over it and enable the Border Patrol to arrive on time to make the arrest.

Even a wall that slowed down illegal immigrants would be helpful. Often when I rode with the Border Patrol, we were just too late to apprehend illegal aliens spotted by cameras or motion detectors. And if we didn't catch them, sometimes worse things awaited them at the hands of the coyotes who hid them in safe houses while they shook down their families for more money.

CHAPTER 5

SAFE HOUSES

After crossing the Rio Grande, illegal aliens are led by a cartel-paid foot guide, who can make a thousand dollars or more per night leading groups of five to fifteen illegals. (On average, a foot guide received one hundred dollars per alien he brought into the United States.)

Because the United States won't prosecute juvenile foreign nationals, the foot guides are often minors. These are the kids in Nuevo Laredo who, flush with cash, are buying the newest sneakers and the most expensive cars. When we did arrest these kids, instead of prosecuting them, we simply handed them over to Mexican authorities, who would release them back to the streets, where they were free to continue working as foot guides for the cartels. We could catch one on Monday, turn him over on Tuesday, and arrest him again on Wednesday. The good news is that because many of these kids become addicted to their high salaries, they continue working as foot guides after turning eighteen—allowing us to prosecute them.

Usually, the foot guides had vehicles waiting for their "cargo" either at the riverbank or as much as forty miles away. The most coveted territory was adjacent to border towns like Laredo, where illegals could be hidden quickly. The more quickly illegal aliens were smuggled into safe houses, the lower the chance that they would be apprehended by the Border Patrol. But most of the land adjacent to the river belonged to ranchers, which meant that in most cases, aliens had to walk many miles through harsh terrain to get to their waiting vehicles. During the summer, the heat in Texas can get to 120 degrees. Aliens trekking across these ranch lands cannot possibly carry enough water with them, so they rely on water left out for cattle (which is often not fit for human consumption) and are extremely vulnerable to dehydration, heat exhaustion, heat stroke, and dying from exposure—especially if they are children. In court, I would constantly hear Border Patrol agents talking about the latest bodies they had found in the desert. And on at least one occasion, Judge Kazen gave a Guatemalan defendant from Group 2 a sentence of only fifteen days because the defendant had seen his cousin die in the desert. Judge Kazen thought that this might be enough to deter him from repeating his offense.

Ranchers told me how they were robbed, beaten, or burglarized by illegal aliens, saw them peeking through a child's bedroom window, or had their property vandalized by them. I prosecuted cases where smugglers had driven right through a rancher's fence or cut through his gates, which often meant not just extensive property damage, but also the possible loss of cattle. Many not only suffered property damage, but also had direct threats made against their lives. The Border Patrol works hard to maintain good relationships with the ranchers, and Border Patrol agents would often help them repair fences or other damage done by illegal aliens. For the Border Patrol, ranchers are invaluable resources. They provide information and access to their property so that the Border Patrol can better conduct its operations. Naturally, through threats and attempted intimidation, the cartels do what they can to discourage the ranchers from being willing to talk to the Border Patrol.

■ ■ ■

Border Patrol agents are trained in tracking people through the desert. They read footprints, examine broken branches and litter, and follow the stench of body odor and other signs that betray the recent presence of illegal immigrants. Almost always, the Border Patrol agents are outnumbered by the illegal aliens they track; if the group scatters, the agents make a priority of tracking and arresting the foot guide. But they also try to prevent groups from scattering by surrounding them. They do this not only so they can make the arrests, but also because any illegals they miss are at grave risk of getting lost and dying in the desert.

Illegal aliens take flight in 95 percent of their encounters with the Border Patrol, and nearly every illegal alien resists arrest, which is the reverse of what happens in normal law enforcement. It is rare for American criminals to resist arrest, and when they do, it is expected that prosecutors will bring down the hammer and that judges will order stiff sentences. In Virginia, for instance, assault on a law enforcement officer is an automatic felony with a six-month minimum sentence. On the border, however, physical assault against law enforcement is the rule and not the exception. Illegal alien assaults on Border Patrol agents who are trying to make arrests are so routine (and so unlikely to be prosecuted because of the already overwhelming burden on the courts) that most agents wouldn't even mention these assaults in their reports unless they suffered serious injuries.

One of the few times we prosecuted an illegal immigrant for assaulting a Border Patrol agent occurred after the alien held the agent under water in the Rio Grande, nearly drowning him. Even after he was rescued from drowning, the agent was still in great danger of dying from disease after swallowing the contaminated water of the Rio Grande and inhaling it into his lungs. Despite having nearly killed a member of law enforcement, the illegal alien was sentenced to only five years in prison.

■ ■ ■

The foot guide's job was done once he delivered the illegal aliens to the vehicle that would transport them to a safe house. Now the driver took over.

Drivers were paid about $250 dollars per alien. So if the driver had a seven-seat SUV and filled it with twelve aliens, he could make $3,000 for just a few hours of driving. Under federal sentencing guidelines, the risk involved between eleven and thirty-six months in prison, if caught. By contrast, we prosecuted a woman with no previous criminal record who, facing home-lessness, had accepted two thousand dollars to drive eighteen kilograms of meth across the border. She was sentenced to eight years in prison. There's far less legal risk (and more money) in trafficking people than in trafficking drugs.

But human traffickers often made their sentences worse by adding on to their offenses. For example, we had several high-speed chases per week—just another accepted fact of life on the border.

These chases were among the most dangerous situations we faced because they posed a danger not just to Border Patrol agents, the smugglers, and illegal aliens, but also to American motorists. The smugglers' vehicles, which were usually vans, SUVs, or pickup trucks, were hard to handle at speeds of more than one hundred miles per hour, and accidents were frequent. Of course, these smugglers rarely had auto insurance, which meant that if they collided with any unlucky motorists, there was little chance of getting the repair costs reimbursed.

I was with Border Patrol agents when they were called to the scene of an auto wreck involving a Honda Pilot that had been going one hundred miles per hour in an area where the speed limit was sixty-five. The Honda Pilot had clipped the front of a pickup truck, tipped onto its side, and slid into the desert dirt, knocking over a barbed-wire fence and leaving a horrid trail of broken glass and blood. In the wreckage, I saw bottles of water and Pedialyte, a child's coloring book, and some baby socks. Two injured illegals were taken into custody (their injuries were too severe for them to get away), but the driver and the others had fled into the desert brush, where there are plenty of places to hide—and, unfortunately, die.

■ ■ ■

It wasn't just accidents and high-speed chases that we were worried about. Sometimes, smugglers would use their vehicles as weapons, attempting to strike Border Patrol agents.

In one instance, I had a case that involved three cars—a decoy vehicle (traffickers often used these to try to distract the Border Patrol), a smuggling vehicle, and what we might call a weaponized car.

The decoy vehicle was driven erratically, violating multiple traffic laws until Border Patrol agents came in pursuit. When the Border Patrol tried to pull the decoy driver over, he ignored their signal and kept going for miles, but at a low speed. That was when the Border Patrol realized it was probably following a decoy. The smuggling vehicle was a Ford Expedition that was already under surveillance because it was riding very low to the ground, as if overloaded, and the driver had violated multiple traffic laws. As a Border Patrol vehicle pursued it with lights and sirens on, a red Hyundai Elantra came screeching out from a gas station, nearly striking the Border Patrol vehicle. The pursuit continued, and a few miles later, the Hyundai pulled in front of the Border Patrol vehicle again and braked suddenly. Fortunately, the Border Patrol driver swerved around it. And in the end, the agents were able to stop all three vehicles. The Ford Expedition was not only filled with illegal aliens, but it was driven by an unlicensed fourteen-year-old illegal alien.

■ ■ ■

Assuming the drivers made it to their safe houses without incident, their job was done. The safe houses varied from houses to apartments to cheap hotels. We had one case where twenty-four illegal aliens were found in a one-bedroom apartment, where they had subsisted on one or two meals a day of beans and water. One of the senior prosecutors in my office said that the only thing about that case which surprised her was that the aliens were given two meals a day instead of just one.

Safe houses are where illegal aliens are kept until the smugglers arrange transport through the last layer of border security: the interior checkpoint. It's also where illegal aliens are held hostage while the smugglers demand the remainder of their fees. If an illegal alien's family has already paid, the cartel might suddenly spring an additional "release fee" and charge exorbitant rates for any food consumed.

In one case I handled, the Laredo Police Department, on the basis of a tip-off, had discovered that a motel room in Laredo was being used as a safe house and that illegal aliens were being held at gunpoint while the cartels tried to extort more money from their relatives. We had many cases like this. What made this case memorable was that the illegal aliens had overheard the defendant—the gunman holding the illegal immigrants hostage—talking to another smuggler about torturing an illegal alien so they could get additional money beyond the usual smuggling and release fees. Based on what the illegal aliens had said, he was a pathetic little pervert who had wanted to do terrible, disgusting things to them. He also had one of the longest juvenile criminal records that I had ever seen, with multiple felonies, assaults, and drugs charges. This was his fourth arrest in the past twelve months alone, and he had gotten little more than a slap on the wrist so far. Now he was facing charges of abduction, kidnapping, human trafficking, usage of a firearm, and torture conspiracy.

But when I talked to a Homeland Security Investigations agent, he told me that as bad as the kid was, he was cooperating with investigators and could be essential to arresting other—and much worse—members of the smuggling ring. I was skeptical, but I deferred to the agent and decided not to oppose bond for the defendant and instead privately briefed the defense attorney and judge about my reasoning. The judge, despite the severity of the charges, agreed. But what this episode revealed to me was just how bad things were on the border—that however bad a thug's record was, it didn't take long to find one even worse.

CHAPTER 6

ARRIVING AT THE INTERNAL CHECKPOINT

Interior immigration checkpoints are within fifty miles of the border. The Laredo checkpoint twenty miles north of town on I-395 conducts more checks than any other immigration checkpoint in the country. It has concrete barriers, cameras, license plate readers, K9 units, and even X-ray machines capable of scanning large cargo trucks (though only a tiny fraction are actually X-rayed).

These checkpoints are the riskiest part of a smuggler's journey, and drivers are compensated extremely well. The standard price from Laredo to San Antonio was one thousand dollars per illegal alien trafficked through the interior checkpoint. This meant that a truck driver with an eighteen-wheeler could make up to sixty thousand dollars in a single trip by transporting sixty people. At the truck depots around Laredo, members of cartels and HSOs literally walk around trying to recruit drivers. At the checkpoint, Border Patrol agents ask drivers, "Are you a U.S. citizen?"

Most drivers say they are, and unless they act suspiciously, look nervous, avoid eye contact, speak no English, or cannot answer simple questions, they are waved through.

If someone in the car admits that he's not a U.S. citizen, he'll be asked to show a visa or some other document showing that he has a legal right to be in the country. Many illegal immigrants use forged or stolen documents—typically passports, driver's licenses, and birth certificates. Some forgeries were laughably absurd, others were quite sophisticated, though Border Patrol agents were adept at spotting minor discrepancies that indicated a forged or stolen document. Under normal circumstances, this process takes less than a minute. It's annoying but not very invasive. However, if something unusual is detected that arouses reasonable suspicion, the vehicle is directed to a "secondary" location.

The "secondary" location is where vehicles are directed for a more thorough search. A Border Patrol agent and a sniffer dog might stroll by. The dogs are adept at sniffing out not just drugs, but also hidden illegal aliens. Another agent might search the vehicle or have it X-rayed. Law enforcement cannot forcibly detain anyone without reasonable suspicion as a matter of law. So when a law enforcement officer has nothing but a hunch, he'll ask permission to perform a search—and usually receive it. I was amazed at how many drivers carrying drugs or illegal immigrants consented to having their cars searched. Perhaps they thought cooperation would lessen the offense.

When I was traveling north, Border Patrol agents sometimes asked permission to search the trunk of my vehicle. I always gave the same response: "No, thank you. I do not consent to any searches or seizures." Whenever I did this, the Border Patrol agent didn't show the slightest disappointment but simply said I could proceed and waved me through.

Even though I wasn't doing anything illegal, I would never consent to a search. For starters, I just wanted to continue my journey and didn't feel like being held up. In addition, I was driving a rental, and I had no idea what little things might have been left behind by previous renters. As a criminal defense attorney back in Richmond, I'd dealt with many cases where people sharing vehicles wound up in trouble because another person had left behind firearms, ammo, marijuana, cocaine, crack, meth, or other contraband in the car. Even if I had done nothing wrong, I could still end up having a very bad day because of someone else, and I wasn't above worrying that a dishonest cop or agent—maybe bought by the cartels—would plant something in my car. Paranoia comes from experience as a criminal defense attorney because you know that bad things happen all the time.

Sometimes, smugglers directed to the secondary location would try to play it cool and drive in that general direction at a normal speed before casually veering back toward the highway. Others would take off at high speeds. Border Patrol agents always had vehicles standing by in case they had to give chase. Smugglers faced harsher sentencing than the aliens (who might be detained as material witnesses) and had much more to lose if they were caught, especially if they were indebted to a cartel.

Usually, these high-speed chases took place on highways. Sometimes they ran onto adjacent ranches, plowing through fences. Sometimes they were on city streets, where the driver would suddenly stop, order the aliens out, and then drive off, hoping the fleeing aliens would distract the Border Patrol. In one case, our office prosecuted a kid who fled an immigration checkpoint in his Honda Civic, speeding up to 132 miles per hour. The aliens inside pleaded with him to let them out, so he stopped his car and did exactly that. Then he got back on the interstate and continued driving at high speeds. He might have gotten away with it because the Border Patrol vehicles were unable to keep up, except that agents radioed ahead and placed spikes that punctured his tires.

Of the two aliens who had been in the car, one got away; the other was captured and told us he was eighteen. After learning that we wanted to detain him as a material witness against the driver, he changed his story and said he was seventeen. I confirmed with the Guatemalan Embassy that he was, in fact, seventeen. We dismissed the detainer on him, and he was deported. Because we had no witnesses, the charge against the driver had to be amended from human smuggling to the lesser offense of fleeing a checkpoint, for which he was sentenced to just probation.

One evening when I was at the checkpoint observing, the driver of an eighteen-wheeler was waived to bring her vehicle up. The Border Patrol expected her to stop so they could make their normal checks. To their surprise, she didn't stop but kept going, heading back onto the highway. A Border Patrol agent and I ran to his vehicle, got in, and took off at high speed to catch up with her. Shootings are rare during or after high-speed chases, but they are known to happen, and I was putting on a Kevlar vest just in case. Right at the peak of excitement, our chase abruptly terminated as the woman quickly brought her truck to a stop. As it turns out, she had just been confused and had thought the Border Patrol agent had waived her through the checkpoint. Such false alarms were surprisingly common.

■ ■ ■

Interior immigration checkpoints remain controversial, both politically and legally.

The legal issue centers on the Fourth Amendment to the Constitution, which states: "The right of the people to be secure in their persons, houses, papers, and effects, against unreasonable searches and seizures, shall not be violated, and no Warrants shall issue, but upon probable cause, supported by Oath or affirmation, and particularly describing the place to be searched, and the persons or things to be seized."

In 1976, the Supreme Court upheld the constitutionality of interior checkpoints in a seven-to-two ruling. The court said these checkpoints constituted reasonable search and seizure under the Fourth Amendment and were easily justified by the substantial public interest in stopping illegal immigration.

Prior to my time in Laredo, I had been strongly opposed to interior checkpoints, believing that they violated the Fourth Amendment. But after seeing them in operation, I'm not so sure. On the one hand, I still believe stopping Americans traveling in their own country without any suspicion of wrongdoing is inherently un-American. It strikes me as wrong, both morally and legally. On the other hand, I have witnessed firsthand the vital role that these checkpoints play in law enforcement operations—not just in preventing illegal immigration, but also in intercepting massive quantities of deadly drugs. Nearly every day I was in court, I handled prosecutions that would not have been possible without these checkpoints.

These checkpoints serve a humanitarian role, as well. We saved many people—including children—from human traffickers and saved the lives of illegal immigrants who were crammed into trailers or trunks in 115-degree heat and were suffering from dehydration and heat exhaustion. The Border Patrol station near Laredo must be one of Gatorade's biggest customers

CHAPTER 7

DETENTION FACILITIES

Laredo's main Border Patrol detention facility is about a fifteen-minute drive from the courthouse and can hold slightly more than two hundred people.

Arrested illegal aliens are taken to a secure entrance at the back of the building and walk down an air-conditioned hallway to a waiting area where they are given drinks and snacks while their personal effects—cash, rings, IDs, and so on—are itemized and secured (usually in a single, gallon-sized Ziploc bag). They are given a receipt for their personal items; none of this is tracked digitally. While I was touring the Laredo facility, I saw some of these bags and wondered—given that the illegals had next to no cash—what they were supposed to do if they got separated from their coyotes. But I guess that was the point—they are completely dependent on them, which gives the coyotes leverage and control.

With their personal effects secured, the aliens are then brought to a main room in the detention area where there are about twenty computers, each manned by a Border Patrol agent who assists with processing. As part of processing, the agents pull together a detailed record for each arrested alien. Because many illegal aliens lack photo IDs or other documents—and will lie about their name, age, family status, and country of origin—biometric data is crucial in linking them to existing records that can reveal past criminal history, deportations, or outstanding warrants. If crimes were committed in the United States, they can be easily found. If they were committed in another country, it can be much harder, though in my time in Laredo we did prosecute one gang member who had illegally crossed the border shortly after serving a twenty-one year murder sentence in El Salvador!

Every arrested illegal alien is read his Miranda Rights in both English and Spanish. Most aliens readily confessed to illegal entry because they wanted to expedite their return home. Their statements were recorded in their "A-Files," which were terrific sourcebooks on how the coyotes operated, what they charged, and why the illegal immigrants had come to the United States in the first place. Almost invariably, their stated motivations were to find work, join with family, or escape violence in their native country. Most said that they had no fear of returning home, but those who did requested asylum (which is a separate matter from the crime of illegal entry), and we prosecuted them for illegal entry as their asylum requests were initiated. As part of the processing, U.S. Immigration and Customs Enforcement (ICE) would place a detainer on each alien. This meant that even if I had to dismiss the criminal charges, the alien would simply be transferred to ICE custody and, in most cases, would be deported.

On a typical day, about 70–80 percent of the illegal aliens arrested in our sector were processed here. Those who weren't were either known juveniles, family units, or certain types of criminals. When I visited the facility in August 2018, it had processed eighteen thousand people so far that year. Once an illegal alien was arrested, we had a seventy-two-hour window to get a defendant in front of a magistrate judge. If we could not meet that requirement, we would simply have them deported without prosecution.

This created a perverse situation. We were so overwhelmed by the number of people crossing the border illegally that we could not process them all in seventy-two hours. As a result, the more people we caught, the less likely we were to prosecute them. Our priority was to prosecute hardened criminals and repeat offenders, but we had to deport 70 percent of arrested illegal aliens without charges.

Lining the walls of the processing room are detention cells, including a couple of small cells set aside for families with juveniles or unaccompanied minors. Those cells could also be used for gang members who had to be separated from rivals; otherwise, they would fight to the death.

Normally, everyone brought in before ten o'clock at night would be processed and ready for court the next day, and juveniles could never be held for more than twenty-four hours. But if someone was brought in over the weekend, they had to wait until Monday to appear in court.

I felt terrible for anyone who had to sit there through the weekend because these cells were intended for temporary detentions. There were no cots—and apparently when the Border Patrol tried providing the aliens with mattresses, they were quickly torn apart—so the aliens were issued disposable blankets instead.

Even though cleaning crews mopped the cells twice a day, the rooms stank. There weren't any showers, towels, laundry facilities, or spare clothes for the illegal aliens. Congressmen who visited the facility, I was told, often asked about this, blaming the Border Patrol for failing to provide adequate facilities. Border Patrol agents responded by informing Congress that they would love to have better facilities and amenities and merely needed Congress to provide the funding. Somehow, that funding never arrived. Despite all of the political posturing from members of Congress about the quality of the facilities, they never vote to actually do anything about it. During my six months in Laredo, no congressman—or even a member of a congressman's staff—came to see what we were dealing with. And because federal regulations require showers and other amenities for people detained longer than seventy-two hours, the Border Patrol sometimes had to rent space at the county jail or even at a nearby hotel. Border Patrol agents told me they had spent half a million dollars on such accommodations so far that year.

As a defense attorney, I've visited clients in numerous jails, and at this facility, I witnessed Border Patrol agents treating inmates with the sort of dignity and humanity that any honest defense attorney would applaud. These meager, temporary facilities are not happy places, but they work as a stopgap until aliens can be brought to court, where the vast majority plead guilty and are either deported or sent to a prison. The people who work in these detention centers deserve our thanks and a lot more funding so they can do more for our country and for the illegal aliens.

CHAPTER 8

IN SEARCH OF THE GRAIL—JOBS, JOBS, JOBS

The overwhelming majority of illegal immigrants come to the United States to find work. In fact, most already have jobs lined up because of family members who paid their smuggling fees. Of the illegal immigrants we prosecuted (we rarely had the resources to prosecute their sponsors or employers), most were heading to jobs in agriculture, construction, restaurant service, or domestic work.

Economically, illegal immigrants have much to gain and little to lose. Most of the illegal immigrants I prosecuted came from Mexico, Guatemala, Honduras, or Bangladesh, where the average annual income ranges from about $1,400 to $8,600. In the United States, working in a restaurant, in agriculture, or in construction could offer an annual salary of between $20,000 and $30,000, a better quality of life, and many more economic opportunities. If the bill for smuggling an illegal alien is $6,000 and that alien makes $20,000 a year in a dishwashing job in the

United States, that means more than a 300 percent return on investment in one year.

Not all illegal immigrants are without skills or work experience. Some told us they had lined up supervisory positions at construction sites, in restaurants, or with landscaping crews—jobs that might pay between $40,000 and $50,000 per year.

The highest-paid illegal alien I encountered was a restaurant manager who told us he was making $70,000 per year. He said he had entered the United States illegally at age fourteen and had become a dishwasher. At the restaurant, he learned to speak English, worked hard, and got a series of promotions. Unfortunately for him, he was deported because of a DUI conviction— but he knew his high-paying job was waiting for him when he could sneak back across the border.

Of course, not only are their own economic prospects better in the United States, but the money they are able to send home to Mexico or Central American countries is extremely valuable to the economies of those countries—which is why those governments have so little incentive to discourage illegal immigration to the United States. Mexico, however, does have an incentive to stop Central American immigrants from crossing into the United States because those immigrants are potentially taking jobs from Mexican immigrants. President Donald Trump has cleverly played on Mexico's national interest to win more Mexican cooperation against illegal immigration from Central America. When President Trump says he has received more cooperation from Mexico than he has from Congress in trying to enforce our border, you can see his point while acknowledging the exaggeration.

■ ■ ■

During my time in Laredo, I often reflected on how extraordinarily fortunate I was to have been born in a country where jobs and opportunities are plentiful—and to a family that valued education and hard work. I heard many illegal aliens refer to the United States as the "land of plenty." Very few, I believe, came here with an intention to commit crimes beyond their initial act of illegal entry. With many, their desire for a job overlapped significantly with their desire to be with their family members already in the United States.

Sometimes an illegal immigrant's family from Mexico would attend the guilty pleas of their loved one who had been arrested for illegally entering the United States. Having family members show up in court often had an impact on judges because it put the defendant in a broader context.

In one case, we prosecuted a twenty-three-year-old woman who had been arrested while swimming across the Rio Grande. She was one of the few who was willing to risk her life by not paying the cartels. It turned out that she had previously entered the country legally with a tourist visa, but she had violated its terms by taking two jobs waitressing at Mexican restaurants in Laredo. Her visa had been revoked—hence her need to come here illegally.

Her mother legally came over from Nuevo Laredo to be in court for her, and the public defender included her in his statement to the court, which focused on the fact that the defendant had merely come to America looking for work.

As usual when defendants pleaded guilty, I chose not to make any sentencing arguments and personally was relieved when the judge sentenced her to time served. The defendant had gone through a lot in just the arrest and booking process, and her mother sat in the court tearful and worried (I even brought her a box of tissues).

We had the names of both restaurants that had employed the young woman illegally, but we never followed up on those leads because we lacked the time, money, and investigators to do it properly. But it was clear to me that the only way to curtail illegal immigration is to go after the employers, and that is rarely done. Jobs attract illegal immigrants. Everything would change dramatically if those jobs were strictly reserved for American citizens and legal aliens and if businesses that employed illegals were seriously punished for doing so. Then—and only then— would we be able to secure our border successfully and stop the humanitarian crisis that currently exists there as the cartels prey on the innocent, dangerous criminals slip past us, and we are overwhelmed by masses of job-seekers from south of the border.

CHAPTER 9

THE DACA DILEMMA

My introduction to DACA came early in my deployment in the form of a bond hearing.

The defendant, whom I'll call "Raul," was a twenty-year-old former DACA recipient who had been charged with human smuggling. I say "former" DACA recipient because any protections he might have had under DACA were rescinded the moment he was charged with a felony. From a legal perspective, Raul was no different than any other illegal alien who had been caught in the United States and charged with a serious crime.

DACA, or Deferred Action for Childhood Arrivals, has been one of the most divisive immigration issues in our country since President Barack Obama initiated the program via executive order in 2012. The intent of the program might have been laudable—protecting people who arrived in this country as the children of illegal immigrant parents—but it has had the unexpected consequence of encouraging illegal immigrants, who hope DACA protections will someday be extended to their children, to bring children with them across the border. But as matter of law, President Obama's imposition of DACA seems blatantly unconstitutional. The way the U.S. federal government is set up, Congress makes laws and the president faithfully executes those laws. The problem with DACA is that President Obama unilaterally created this program; the president—and not Congress—wrote a law that conflicted with existing federal laws while simultaneously stating that he would not execute the duly enacted laws of Congress.

What is particularly tragic about many of these DACA recipients—whose parents brought them unlawfully into this country—is that they grew up without any legal status as an American citizen, yet they feel "American." After all, they grew up here. Some of them came here very young, have no memory of their country of origin, and attended our public schools and universities. Some of them only learned of their lack of legal status after getting into what normally would be considered minor legal trouble or when they applied to college. In court, many of these DACA recipients did not wear translation headphones because English was their first and, in at least one case, only language. When DACA recipients are charged with crimes and enter state or federal custody, ICE places detainers on them, which means that if they leave custody of the U.S. Marshals for any reason (such as bond or even dismissal of the charges that caused them to lose their DACA status in the first place), they are transferred to ICE for deportation. Of the DACA recipients I encountered, the prospect of deportation terrified them more than prison because deportation meant being separated from their families and sent to what is now to them a foreign country.

There is strong public debate today over what should happen to DACA recipients. What is *not* up for debate is that the situation they are in is grossly unfair. In almost every case, they bear no fault or responsibility for their lack of legal status. President Obama encouraged Congress to resolve the situation permanently by enacting a resolution to create a DACA-like program, and when Congress failed, he took unilateral action by creating DACA himself. Congress continues to do nothing to fix the problem. Although Congress let President Obama impose DACA, it now works in conjunction with activist judges to prevent President Trump from undoing this usurpation of congressional authority and enforcing our immigration laws as written by Congress!

DACA amounts to a federal executive order *not* to deport persons unlawfully brought into the country as children. By applying to be part of the DACA program, those who are accepted receive legal status to remain in the United States—even if they are not citizens. To be eligible for DACA, a person must have entered the United States before the age of sixteen, have completed or currently be enrolled in school, and not have committed any significant crimes. There is also a $465 fee, as well as a few other criteria.

Regardless of whether one agrees with the *policy* behind DACA, as a matter of *law* it is almost certainly unconstitutional, and on those grounds President Trump canceled the program shortly after taking office (although legal challenges have kept it in place, at least temporarily). DACA would be perfectly legal if the legislation came from Congress, but under the Constitution, a president can't create programs like this on his own.

The reason why it is unconstitutional is because Article I of the Constitution gives Congress the responsibility to make laws, and Article II gives the president the duty to execute the laws enacted by Congress to the best of his ability. The president must enforce the laws of the nation, regardless of whether he agrees with them. Presidents and prosecutors alike do not get to pick and choose the laws they will follow and enforce. The law is the law, and we all must follow it until it is changed. Furthermore, the president lacks the power to create laws, and enacting a program like DACA was tantamount to the president rewriting immigration laws, rather than enforcing the current immigration laws.

During my time in Laredo, I did my job and prosecuted these cases. But personally, there were times when I found them heartbreaking. The job of a prosecutor is to do more than just enforce the law; it is to do justice, and I did not feel justice was being served when it came to cases against former DACA recipients. I had to do my duty, but I also felt that it was well past time for Congress to do its duty. Its failure to both reform our immigration laws and support the president in his enforcement of them is not just a scandal; it is a tragedy.

Balancing my personal beliefs with my duty as a U.S. prosecutor was put to the test at Raul's bond hearing.

While it sounds terrible that Raul was charged with human smuggling, not all cases are equally horrific. In fact, this was one of the least offensive cases I had encountered. A friend had offered Raul $350 to drive four illegal aliens in his sedan from Laredo to San Antonio—easy money for a four-hour round trip. Because he had fewer than five people in his vehicle, he would not have been charged with a crime if he had been a U.S. citizen instead of an illegal alien. We knew from license plate checks that he had never made this drive before, and we also knew he was not part of any organized crime syndicate. (If he had been, he would have known the going rate was a thousand dollars per person! Clearly, Raul had been taken advantage of for his ignorance.)

For a case like this, we would normally set bond at seventy-five thousand dollars, but we would only require one thousand dollars to be secured—meaning that one thousand dollars would be all the person would have to pay to be released from jail while his case was pending. Unfortunately for Raul, Pretrial Services had recommended that he be held without bond because of his lack of legal status in the United States.

As a matter of policy, any foreign national legally or illegally in the United States is held without bond. The rationale is that because the defendant is not an American citizen, he is inherently a flight risk because he could return to his home country to avoid prosecution. This is a fair assessment in most cases, especially when the case involves illegal immigrants who have arrived from Mexico, given that the border is just a three-minute jog from the courthouse.

Raul's case was an exception to this rule—or at least it should have been. Although he was technically a Mexican national and an illegal alien, I realized after reviewing his history that there was no cause for concern; Raul wouldn't try to flee from the United States. I also felt it was unjust for him to be treated any differently than a U.S. citizen charged with the same crime. To my mind, he should have been given a bond just like any U.S. citizen charged with the same offense.

I did some background checking and learned that when Raul was only sixteen months old, his mother had fled an abusive husband in Mexico. It appears that Mexican authorities had been unwilling or unable to do anything about the violent husband. Raul's mother took her three children illegally across the border into the United States. In the eighteen years since, the entire family had lived in Laredo and had never set foot back in

Mexico. At the time of his arrest, Raul still lived in the same house with his mom, two sisters, and stepfather.

Raul had a clean criminal history for his entire life—not even a traffic violation. In fact, he had a promising future, since he had recently graduated from high school and was enrolled in the local community college for the coming fall. He held a part-time job at his stepfather's construction company and was eager to get ahead in life. Rather than live in the shadows, he had applied for and was enrolled in the DACA program, which had protected him from deportation. But he lost these protections when he made the stupid decision to drive a few illegal aliens up to San Antonio. Now he faced losing everything by being deported to Mexico.

Raul was distraught. He had no connection to his country of birth and had always considered himself an American.

What particularly stung me about this case was that Raul's lack of legal status was not his fault; it was his mother's fault. She had broken the law by bringing him here illegally. As a child, Raul had paid the price, having been forced to grow up in a country where he had no legal status. I could see his mother sitting in the back of the courtroom with her new husband and Raul's two older sisters.

It was the U.S. Attorney's Office's policy to oppose bond for illegal aliens and other foreign nationals. In fact, in every case I had seen so far where an illegal alien had been charged with human smuggling, the defendant had simply waived the bond hearing because he knew he didn't have a chance of being granted bond by the judge. But I didn't think that was right, at least not in this case. As a matter of law, a bond is to be given to any defendant unless he or she is deemed a flight risk or a danger to the community.

In my analysis of Raul's case, I could not come up with a coherent argument that he posed any such risks. If he had been a United States citizen—and I noted his lack of citizenship was not his fault—he would almost certainly have been granted bond. As such, I decided to violate our policy and support a reasonable bond. I knew I might have some explaining to do, but I figured I had a decent argument.

While Judge Kazen worked his way through a long list of mass guilty pleas for illegal entry, I scanned the courtroom for Raul's public defender. I finally located the attorney, whom I'll call "Frank," an elderly, distinguished-looking gentleman. We shook hands, he gave me a close look, and he asked, "Are you new here?" As a former defense attorney, I knew exactly what he was thinking: Lacking the perspective that comes with real-world experience, new prosecutors have a tendency to be overly aggressive, rigid, and overall unreasonable. While their inexperience is an advantage to the defense attorney when it comes to a trial, new prosecutors are challenging when it comes to negotiating plea bargains because they view every minor offense as a major one, making mountains out of molehills. Frank, already prepared for his client to have a bad morning in court, thought it was about to get even worse.

I explained that I was a special prosecutor and an Army Judge Advocate who was brought to Laredo to assist the understaffed U.S. Attorney's Office. Frank looked at me even more sourly than before because military lawyers have a reputation for inflexibility. At the time, I didn't know if Frank was a good lawyer (turns out he was), but he sure didn't have a good poker face.

I told him I had just read Raul's file and wanted to know if he planned to waive the bond hearing. Frank hesitated for a moment, then said that he wanted a bond hearing, even though he knew it was unlikely that bond would be granted. He had the hangdog look of a defense attorney who knows he has a losing case, but still has to go through the motions.

I told Frank I'd been impressed by Raul's background report—his education, length of time in the country, and employment. Frank looked surprised and decided to share more information, possibly because he saw an opening. He described Raul's strong connections to the Laredo community and his lack of connections to Mexico.

I nodded and said, "That's why I'm not opposed to bond." Frank was clearly surprised, but I saw no point in being coy. "Raul has no ties to Mexico, he's not a danger or a flight risk, and I don't see any reason for him to be held without bond." Frank shook my hand and said he'd talk to Raul's family members, who were seated on benches in the back of the court.

By the time our case was called, Frank had already spoken with the court clerk, who had passed word to the judge that the government was not opposed to a bond.

Because Raul was an illegal alien, Judge Kazen looked puzzled by this unusual development. I explained, "The government does not object to a reasonable bond that will allow the defendant to continue living at home with his mother and sisters and continue working his job here in Laredo."

Frank took it from there, emphasizing that his client had been a DACA recipient, although he acknowledged Raul's DACA status was now questionable in light of the charges. Judge Kazen said he'd take the matter under advisement and that, for the moment, he would defer the decision to grant or deny bond. Meanwhile, Raul would continue to be held without bond.

Sadly, Raul never got his bond. A few days after the bond hearing, Frank and I conferred privately with Judge Kazen at the bench. Frank said he hadn't realized that when a DACA recipient is charged with a felony—*even if not convicted*—he automatically loses his DACA status and all the protections against deportation that come with it.

Because of this, an immigration hold (ICE detainer) had been placed on Raul, which meant that if he was given bond, ICE would pick him up and hold him in custody until he was deported. This was a learning experience for all of us, and I had to oppose giving a bond to Raul or any DACA recipient—however reluctantly. Toward the end of my deployment in Laredo, we did finally find a way to get bond for some former DACA recipients, but it took weeks and was a bureaucratic nightmare.

If Raul had been a U.S. citizen, he would have been convicted—which Raul ultimately was—but likely would have been sentenced to minimal, if any, prison time. Raul, as a former DACA recipient, was deported.

But I knew there was a good chance we would see him again. His life was here in America, so I had no doubt that he would try to reenter the United States illegally.

■ ■ ■

Although most people who cross the border illegally are looking for work (or have jobs waiting for them), the people who try the hardest with the most persistence are those who previously lived here. To them, America is home, and they will undertake grave risks to reunite with their families.

During my six months in Laredo, I saw many former DACA recipients get arrested as they tried to reenter the country illegally after being deported. One case involved a tall, thin, twenty-one-year-old male whom I'll call Tomás.

Tomás caught my attention when he walked into the courtroom because he was the only one of his group pleading guilty to unlawful entry who was not wearing translation headphones. He also appeared to be in good health and was wearing designer clothes. I marked him as a DACA recipient and had a sinking feeling that his case was going to be painful. Unfortunately, I was right.

I grabbed Tomás's A-File from the Border Patrol agent seated beside me and started browsing through it. As I read, I took a deep breath and sighed. Tomás had been brought into the United States illegally by his mother when he was an infant and had grown up in Houston with her and his stepfather, who was a U.S. citizen. Tomás had no idea he was in the country illegally. He graduated from high school and went to work in construction while enrolled at a community college; he was studying to become an engineer. Once he realized he was in the country illegally, he applied for and received DACA status. But he lost it a month beforehand after pleading guilty to a misdemeanor drug charge and serving twenty days in a local jail. As soon as he was released, he was picked up by ICE and deported to Mexico.

Immediately after being deported, Tomás tried to sneak back into the country. He was caught, convicted of illegal entry, and deported again. He immediately tried again and was caught and convicted a second time. According to his statements to Border Patrol, his family then hired cartel-affiliated smugglers to bring him across the border. He was caught after swimming across the Rio Grande. And here he was in court, preparing for his third guilty plea.

Judge Song asked Tomás what he was trying to achieve by returning to the United States. He replied in perfect English, "I'm trying to get back home to my parents." It was hard to ignore that he was now in handcuffs and ankle shackles for what I considered to be perfectly normal behavior: trying to return to the only life he had ever known.

Judge Song paused, and the court was utterly silent. Finally, she asked, "Do you have any family in Mexico? Any grandparents. Any aunts or uncles?"

"My grandparents are dead," Tomás replied. "And my aunts and uncles are all missing." On the border, that's code for: "They were murdered by the cartels."

"Do you know anyone in Mexico?" Judge Song asked.

"No, I know no one."

I was tempted to stand up and say, "Screw it; let him go," and dismiss the charge. Legally, I had the power to do that, but I was also sworn to uphold the law. And even if I dismissed the charge, ICE would still deport him because he was in the country illegally.

"I really do understand why you are trying to come back here," Judge Song said, "but you are not allowed. I know it's not easy, but you need to build a new life for yourself in Mexico. There are good-paying jobs for people like you in Mexico—people who grew up in the United States and know the country very well."

"Well," Tomás said, "I don't really speak Spanish, but I'll do my best, your honor."

At least in this case, Tomás didn't have a wife or kids in the United States. Cases like that came up too with deported former DACA recipients.

Judge Song told Tomás, "You need to stay away from the border. It's not good for you. It will only bring you trouble." She sentenced him to fifteen days in jail (rather than the normal sixty for a repeat offender).

I knew that after he served his fifteen days and was deported, Tomás would try again to rejoin his family. How do I know? Because if I were in his shoes, that's exactly what I'd do.

There are a lot of politicians in Washington who boast about how tough or compassionate they are on immigration, but in the case of DACA, "tough" does not equate to smart, prudent, or moral. And those who tout their own "compassion" have failed to take any effective congressional action to deal with the crisis at the border—and at times even deny that it *is* a crisis, and at other times assert that it is, somehow, a crisis of President Trump's own making because he tried to secure our borders. Law enforcement, the legal system, and the citizens of border towns live with the consequences of our dysfunctional Congress every day.

CHAPTER 10

FAMILY SEPARATION

My time in Laredo coincided with one of the biggest political firestorms of the Trump presidency: a media backlash over the separation of families at the border.

It began when a photo surfaced online of what appeared to be two children in a cage. Stories rippled through the news media about President Trump's alleged brutality. After just a few days, however, it was revealed that the photo had been taken in 2014—when Barack Obama was president. After that, the firestorm over the photo mostly died out.

But a week after that story tamped down, there was another media firestorm. Media outlets reported that illegal immigrant parents and children were being separated after the parents were arrested. The adults were sent to detention facilities while the children were placed with relatives in the United States, in foster care, or in youth homes.

Unlike the "children in cages" story, there was a basis of truth to this one, but not for the reasons spun by politicians and the media. I don't like families being separated, but in America—along with every other civilized country on the planet—when adults are arrested, their children do not go to jail with them. No sane or moral nation locks up children in jails with their parents when their parents are charged or convicted of crimes. Instead, when an adult is arrested (anywhere in the United States) and a child is present, children are sent to live with family members or go to Child Protective Services, which places them in foster homes or in group homes while the parent is in custody. This is the standard procedure across the United States, regardless of whether a person is arrested for a DUI in New York City or an illegal border crossing in Texas.

One of my biggest criticisms of the United States criminal justice system is the long-term damage done to families because of the incarceration of non-violent criminals. As a defense attorney back in Virginia, I witnessed numerous examples of families torn apart over non-violent crimes. In one case, a client received a mandatory minimum sentence of ten days in jail for his third charge of driving with a suspended license. On the day he was arrested, my client had been driving to work (with his license still suspended) to pay the fines and court costs from his previous two convictions so that he could get a license. Because he was jailed and unable to work, he ended up being fired from his job and couldn't pay his rent, which forced him, his son, and his disabled girlfriend into homelessness.

I'm all for punishing misconduct and locking away people who pose a danger to society, but there must be a better and less destructive way of dealing with non-dangerous criminals.

Still, family separation, which is clearly destructive to many innocent people, has long been commonplace in the U.S. justice system. For that reason, I couldn't comprehend the outrage when the news broke of family separations under President Trump. After all, this had been happening in America for years and was an ordinary and accepted practice.

To be fair, what was happening under President Trump was the result of a change in policy—not law. For decades, the law has been clear that when people cross the border illegally, they can be prosecuted for a misdemeanor. Although this law was on the books under past presidents, few border crossers were actually prosecuted. Instead, illegal entry was treated as a civil or administrative matter. People caught entering the United States illegally were—if not immediately deported—given a date to appear at an immigration court. This policy was dubbed "catch and release" because most defendants never showed up for their court dates. Still, when prosecutions did occur under past presidents (Republicans and Democrats), just like now, the families were separated. In my opinion, if Democrats don't like this, they should work to garner enough support to change the laws, rather than criticizing the executive branch for enforcing laws that Congress itself put in place.

The Trump administration issued its "zero tolerance" policy on April 6, 2018, which meant that from then on, everyone who crossed the border illegally would be prosecuted. Because that meant a substantial increase in people being criminally charged instead of being simply deported, this led to a spike in the number of families being separated as a result of parents going to jail. The media's highly charged reporting on this inevitable consequence of enforcing our laws created political turmoil for President Trump.

The administration responded to this avalanche of criticism and attention by quietly issuing a slight change in policy: The Border Patrol would rapidly deport adults who arrived with children. The adults, however, would still be booked and processed to establish a record with biometric data so that we would know if they tried to reenter. Because they were not being prosecuted, their children could remain with them the entire time. We referred to these scenarios as "family situations."

This shift in policy happened shortly before I arrived in Laredo. But as much as I disliked seeing families separated, this new policy troubled me even more, because if illegal aliens knew they wouldn't be prosecuted if they brought children with them, then the United States government had just provided them with a perverse incentive to travel with children. As it turned out, my fears were justified. From the moment this policy was instituted, we saw a steady increase in the number of aliens coming over the border with children in tow.

■ ■ ■

Border Patrol agents knew that if they encountered a "family situation," they were supposed to deport the adults and children together rather than charging the adults with crimes. But sometimes it wasn't that easy, and mistakes were made.

In one case, a Border Patrol agent pulled me aside during court and whispered the dreaded words: "We have a family situation."

I grimaced and asked to see the paperwork. I did not want to deal with a political lightning rod, but the paperwork revealed that we did have a mother, father, and child who had been part of a group caught crossing the border illegally. In accordance with the new policy, the mother and child were kept together and promptly deported, but there had been a mistake: the father had been separated from them. Instead of being deported, he had been charged with illegal entry.

The father had been deported several times previously and also had a criminal history in the United States, including indecent exposure and two drunk driving convictions. His record wasn't bad enough to meet the points criteria for a felony charge, but it was enough to ensure that he would be sentenced to about one hundred days in jail for a misdemeanor conviction.

The Border Patrol agent asked me if he should prepare documents to dismiss the charge. I thought about it, but finally said no. To me, the very fact that he brought his family with him and exposed them to danger just so he could have his get-out-of-jail-free card was a reason *not* to dismiss his charge, and to instead push for a tougher sentence. He was attempting to manipulate the system, and this was no longer a family separation issue because the mother and child were together.

Ultimately, the father pleaded guilty and was sentenced to about a hundred days in jail. Later, I was very glad I hadn't dismissed the charge, because the U.S. Attorney's Office in Laredo received information that the defendant might not have been the child's father, after all; it appeared that he was lying in order to avoid prosecution and deportation.

We had many cases where we had similar suspicions, but, unfortunately, it wasn't feasible for us to do DNA tests to verify every parent-child relationship. In many cases, it wasn't even possible to obtain marriage or birth certificates.

■ ■ ■

One morning in court, we had a young adult girl from Guatemala who had illegally crossed the border with her sixteen-year-old brother. When they were arrested, she asked for asylum and claimed that she was afraid of the gang MS-13, stating (in

Spanish), "Mara Salvatrucha wants to hurt me." I was dubious of her claim because she refused to provide any details or substantiating evidence, nor did she have any explanation for why MS-13 might have threatened her.

Catching adult and juvenile siblings together was very unusual. Because this wasn't the parent-child situation they were more familiar with, the Border Patrol officials didn't treat the brother and sister as a "family situation." Instead, they processed each independently. Because she was an adult, she was prosecuted. As a juvenile unaccompanied by a parent with no relatives that we could locate, the brother was sent to a group home. In these situations, juvenile aliens are sent to the nearest group home with room available—and in this case, that meant Florida. The fact that there were no group homes with vacancies closer to Laredo will give you an idea of just how overwhelmed our system was. Later in my time at the border, we encountered a case where an unaccompanied minor had to be sent to a group home in New Jersey.

In the case of the brother and sister, the public defender for the sister wanted me to dismiss the charge. I considered it, but I ultimately declined because dismissing the charge would not reunite the siblings any faster. Moreover, she had committed a crime by entering the country illegally, and the fact that she brought her younger brother with her didn't make it less of a crime.

She pleaded "not guilty" and asked for a trial. We scheduled a trial thirty days out, but after a few days she changed her mind and entered a guilty plea. Her public defender had no doubt advised her that the criminal charge was unrelated to her asylum request and that it was best to expedite things by pleading guilty.

■ ■ ■

In another case, we prosecuted a fifty-year-old father and his twenty-year-old son for illegal entry. The son was in Group 1 because he had no immigration or criminal history, and the father was in Group 2 because he had been charged with a DUI more than a decade earlier and had been deported. As usual, the defendants in Group 1 entered their mass guilty pleas first and received time served, which meant that they would be deported within a day or two. The father, in Group 2, was likely to be sentenced to fifteen days in jail prior to his deportation.

As always, the defendants could make statements before the sentencing. Most defendants decline this opportunity, but the father apologized for entering the United States illegally and requested that his son be allowed to stay with him while he served his time, mistakenly assuming that he and his son would be receiving the same sentence. The father became distraught and started weeping when the judge explained that his son was getting "time served" and would likely be deported before he finished his jail sentence. The father begged to be deported immediately so he could stay with his son. He appeared fearful, but neither he nor his son had applied for asylum; both had told Border Patrol agents that they had entered the United States to work.

The public defender, while noting this was an unusual request, asked Judge Kazen to sentence the father to time served so that he could be with his son. Judge Kazen turned to me, and although I wasn't thrilled, I said that the government had no objection. It had been over a decade since the father's last prior illegal entry, so I suspected he wasn't about to try again anytime soon. Judge Kazen sentenced the father to time served.

■ ■ ■

While economic opportunity is a powerful motivator for people to enter the United States illegally, nothing is stronger than the love for one's family. Many of the aliens we prosecuted for entering the United States illegally were doing so to be with their children—often conceived and born during a previous period of illegal residence in the United States. During sentencing, I heard hundreds of stories from illegal aliens who tearfully described how desperate they were to be with their wives and children here in the United States.

One day in court, we had two defendants who weren't wearing the translation headphones and spoke perfect English. Although they had not been part of the DACA program, they had been brought into the United States as minors and grew up here. Judge Song asked them about their situation. One of them said he wanted to see his two children in the United States. Judge Song gave her usual response: "I understand your reasons, but that doesn't make it right." By "right," she meant "legal."

Because this man was not allowed in the United States, the only legal way for him to see his children was for his wife to bring them to Mexico. Sometimes, however, the parents are not on good terms, and a judge cannot award shared custody or visitation rights to a parent outside the country.

Another day in court, we had a thirty-eight-year-old Mexican citizen who had been arrested for crossing the border illegally after he was deported. He had lived illegally in Los Angeles for twenty years. During that time, he had married and had five children. In asking for leniency, his public defender pointed out that he had lived in the United States longer than he had lived in Mexico.

In my view, the fact that the defendant had gotten away with committing a crime every day for twenty years was not an argument for leniency—if anything, it was an argument for a harsher sentence. The defendant also had a DUI conviction and a prior illegal entry conviction. Still, the judge found the public defender's argument persuasive and sentenced the man to thirty days in jail instead of the usual sixty, after which time he would be deported—again. I have no doubt that this will not be the last time he tries to enter the United States illegally.

■ ■ ■

In another case, we prosecuted a thirty-two-year-old Guatemalan who had lived in the United States illegally for six years. She had married and had two children in the United States, and her children, by default, were U.S. citizens. Seeing cases like this gave me a bad impression of birthright citizenship, which creates the perverse incentive of encouraging people to enter the United States illegally to have children. In court, many illegal aliens talk openly about their goal of having children who would be U.S. citizens.

My first thought was that her children's welfare was more important than punishing her for trying to be with them. But she had chosen to violate the law and had no one to blame but herself. She was sentenced to sixty days in jail because this was her second attempt to enter the country illegally within a year. There's little doubt that she will try a third time. When a mother is separated from her children, there is no happy ending.

In another case, we prosecuted a mother who had come to the United States three years earlier with her two minor children, who were now six and eight years old. At some point, the mother had gotten a drug conviction and been deported. Her children stayed behind, living with the defendant's sister. The mother asked for leniency, talking about how much she missed her children. Judge Song asked her why her children hadn't come with her to Mexico, and the woman responded that she wanted her children to remain in the United States so they could get a good education. That was a perfectly valid reason, but again, it was no excuse for breaking the law, and her casual assumption that American taxpayers should foot the bill for her children's education grated on me.

■ ■ ■

A Lawful Permanent Resident (LPR), often known as a "green card holder," is a noncitizen authorized to live in the United States permanently. With a few exceptions—such as voting and serving on juries—they have the same rights and responsibilities as U.S. citizens. For instance, they can join the military and are eligible for in-state tuition at public universities. In this case, a green card holder had been arrested for driving across the border and passing off a nine-year-old and seventeen-year-old as her own children. A sharp-eyed Border Patrol officer recognized that the pictures on the passports didn't quite match (she had used her own children's passports for these other children). Although the woman repeatedly affirmed—including in writing—that the children were her own, they weren't.

The seventeen-year-old was a friend's nephew. The woman had agreed to smuggle him across the border as a favor. The nine-year-old had a more involved story. The child's mother had been working at a restaurant in Alabama, sending four hundred dollars a month to a grandmother in Mexico to support the child. However, unbeknownst to the mother, the grandmother's health was failing, and without telling the child's mother, the grandmother had paid for the child to be smuggled into the United States (including five hundred dollars that went to the green card–holding driver). Because we didn't yet know about the mother, the child was placed in foster care in the United States.

Although the green card holder had not entered the country illegally herself, she was still lined up with everyone else entering guilty pleas to illegal entry. Normally when defendants pleaded guilty, I did not make any sentencing arguments; this was part of the unofficial plea bargain (though it might be more accurate to call it a "plea understanding"). However, exceptions were made, especially when children were involved.

In this case, Judge Sheldon was presiding. Before we started processing the mass guilty pleas, I asked him if we could move the green card holder's case to the end for sentencing arguments. The judge looked surprised but agreed.

After everyone else from Groups 1 and 2 had been sentenced and the courtroom had been cleared, I approached the microphone. The public defender also approached with his client beside him. I gave Judge Sheldon a recap of the undisputed facts of the case, pointing out each crime the woman had committed in making false statements to law enforcement by claiming that the children were hers. I reminded Judge Sheldon that while the woman had only been charged with a misdemeanor, she could have been charged with multiple felonies.

I pointed out that in addition to her false statements, she could have been charged with two additional felonies for misusing passports. Finally, I noted that the act of smuggling a child for profit was not only illegal, but also morally depraved. I emphasized how lucky she was not to have one, let alone multiple, felony charges, and instead was facing just a single misdemeanor. I asked Judge Sheldon to sentence her to the maximum of 180 days.

The public defender then offered a rebuttal—and did an outstanding job. Not only did he downplay the seriousness of her crimes, but he also emphasized that in pleading guilty, the woman had taken full responsibility. He noted that she was already facing grave consequences over the misdemeanor conviction: she might lose her green card status and be deported. And he noted that she had been in the United States for twenty years and had no prior criminal history. Lastly, he pointed out that the woman clearly had not realized just how serious an offense she was committing, otherwise she would have demanded a lot more than just five hundred dollars for risking so much.

Judge Sheldon addressed the woman directly. He told her that her crime was a very serious violation of the law. He emphasized how fortunate she was in being charged and sentenced for a misdemeanor and not a felony, which could have resulted in years of prison time. He sentenced her to ninety days, which was half the maximum sentence. But that was far longer than the sentences for most defendants who pleaded guilty to misdemeanor illegal entry.

The woman broke down, sobbing uncontrollably at the thought of spending ninety days in federal prison. Judge Sheldon told her he imposed that sentence to deter her and others from committing similar crimes and reminded her that she was incredibly lucky not to be a convicted felon.

CHAPTER 11

ASYLUM SEEKERS, REFUGEES, AND CARAVANS

When the first caravan of "refugees" marching from Central America was announced shortly before the 2018 midterm elections, our intelligence indicated that it was headed to Laredo. Border Patrol started erecting concertina fencing all along the Rio Grande and making plans to deal with the thousands of people expected to arrive. However, the caravan suddenly changed direction, heading toward Tijuana instead of Laredo. We learned that this change came about because the Laredo cartels, worried that the caravan would interfere with their business, murdered three Hondurans in the caravan, sending a message for the caravan to stay clear of Laredo. It is a dark joke, but it was probably the first time anyone went to Tijuana for safety!

The U.S. Immigration and Naturalization Act defines a refugee as someone who is unable or unwilling to return to his home country because of fear of persecution based on "race, religion, nationality, membership in a particular social group, or political opinion. . . ." This language mirrors that of the United Nations Convention Relating to the Status of Refugees and Protocol Relating to the Status of Refugees (1951 and 1967), which established the international legal definition of a refugee.

Under the principle of "first safe country," asylum seekers are required to apply for refugee status in the first safe country they enter. For example, if a woman flees persecution in Guatemala and heads north, passing through Mexico, the woman is legally required to apply for refugee status in Mexico. She cannot insist on applying for asylum in the United States. Refugees do not get to pick and choose their place of refuge. Asylum is meant to protect people from murder and torture and to save lives; it is not about improving their employment prospects. Refugee law was framed, in large part, as a reaction to the failure to save Jewish refugees from the Holocaust—and it became an international obligation in the wake of World War II.

There is no question today that people throughout the world are still persecuted because of their race or religion. But it is also true that the overwhelming majority of aliens who enter the United States illegally and then claim refugee status are not among them. Instead, illegal immigrants to the United States apply for asylum as a last-ditch effort to stay in the United States, where they hope to find better jobs or be reunited with family members. I know this because that's what the illegal aliens told us; their statements were included in their A-Files.

Legitimate refugees are supposed to arrive at lawful ports of entry and request asylum. This occurred in less than 1 percent of the asylum cases I encountered during my time in Laredo. Instead, in 99 percent of the cases I encountered, the "refugees" first tried to enter the United States illegally and were smuggled across the border by the cartels. It was only after being caught that they decided to request asylum.

Shortly after I finished my assignment in Laredo, President Trump tried to curtail the rampant fraud and abuse within our asylum system. The president announced that those who followed the law and presented themselves at lawful ports of entry could file asylum claims; those who entered the country illegally could not. But a federal judge temporarily blocked the Trump administration's action, ruling that the law makes no distinction between asylum seekers who enter the United States legally or illegally.

■ ■ ■

Illegal immigrants have learned that it often pays to invoke U.S. asylum laws. The numbers bear that out. In 2007, the number of asylum claims was 5,171, according to the Department of Homeland Security. By 2016, the number had had jumped to 91,786—an increase of nearly 1,700 percent!

By law, when a person claims that he fears returning to his home country, he cannot be deported. Instead, an asylum officer is assigned to do what is called a "credible fear" interview. This is meant to determine whether there is a *prima facie* case for a person to be granted asylum—meaning that the standard of proof, at this stage, is very low. If the alien meets this low standard, then the asylum claim progresses to a hearing with an immigration judge. Because of the large backlog of such cases, the wait time is very long, averaging more than a year and a half, according to the group Human Rights First. Even if aliens claim credible fear, they can still be prosecuted for illegal entry. In my notes, I estimated that 20 percent of those we tried for illegal entry claimed credible fear, though in my memory it was a little higher—maybe a third of all cases. Very few Mexicans claimed a credible fear of returning home, while the percentage was much higher for illegal aliens from Central and South America, who, under the "first safe country" rule, should have applied for asylum elsewhere.

Based on my observations, I'm very comfortable saying that 90 percent of those who claimed refugee status were abusing the system and were not legitimate refugees, according to the legal definition. At the national level, about 20 percent of asylum claims processed by the Justice Department are granted, according to government data, which suggests that 80 percent are either fraudulent or fall short of the U.S. standard.

Of course, many Latin American countries suffer from high rates of poverty and crime. Although these are certainly understandable reasons for wanting to leave a country, they do not meet the legal standard for asylum. I certainly feel compassion for people trying to move their families to a more prosperous country with less violence and more economic opportunity, but I strongly believe the asylum process is an inappropriate way for them to do so. Aliens making fraudulent asylum claims contribute to the backlog of cases and delay justice for those with legitimate asylum claims. In my private law practice, I do considerable pro bono work for real refugees who fled for their lives—not to seek economic opportunity. They escaped true horrors and bloodshed, and now they have to wait years while their claims are processed, in part because of the baseless claims being made by those exploiting the system. Examples of such refugees I've helped include interpreters who worked alongside the U.S. military in Iraq and Afghanistan, Christian refugees from Nigeria, and MS-13 victims from Central America.

In many of the asylum cases I encountered, the aliens had flat-out admitted to Border Patrol agents that their real reason for coming to the United States was to look for work or reunite with family members—not to flee any type of persecution.

A common refrain of asylum seekers was that they had to escape a bad neighborhood. What they meant by this was that their homes were dominated by gangs and cartels. But for the six thousand dollars they each paid the cartels to cross the border, they could easily have moved to a safer neighborhood in their own country.

Some of the asylum claims were completely ridiculous. One woman claimed refugee status, saying she feared her hometown police. The Border Patrol agent asked her why she feared them. Because, she said, a police officer had asked her out on a date. The Border Patrol agent asked if the police officer had threatened her or had a reputation for violence or if anything bad had happened. "No," she said. The Border Patrol agent asked her to explain what exactly she feared. The woman shrugged and said nothing.

The aliens who make such ludicrous asylum claims are hoping to benefit from the policy of "catch and release." Because the United States is legally required under U.S. and international law to process all asylum claims, and because there's such a long backlog of cases, many aliens who claim refugee status are released while their cases are pending. Once released, they are free to live in the United States and can work and send money home to their families. They can also establish residency. If they marry a U.S. citizen, they can remain in the United States permanently, even if their asylum claims are later rejected.

These perverse incentives help explain why our asylum system is completely overrun with illegitimate claims.

■ ■ ■

I witnessed all kinds of outrageous antics and terrible fraud being performed by aliens seeking to get into the asylum system and be released.

Family units are more likely to get "catch and release" than single adults, which leads to some aliens creating fake family units. In one case that I prosecuted, a man and woman, claiming to be husband and wife, had presented themselves at a lawful port of entry with two minors aged nine and eleven. They claimed these minors as their own children and even had documentation. They entered an asylum claim.

About a week later, while in ICE custody, the man came forward, saying his conscience had compelled him to speak. He confessed that he and the woman were not married and that he had no familial connection to the minors they had claimed as their children. The children themselves weren't even related to each other, the man said.

The judge and I were both dubious that this man had suddenly discovered his conscience. His public defender privately confided to me that he suspected the man had been overwhelmed after spending a week in a small detention area with two children who were not his; the situation had gotten too real for him. He also might have realized that being recognized as the children's father during the asylum process could create problems for him down the road. In court, this man did look genuinely worried and did show remorse. He even teared up. The woman, his fake wife, came to court with a very different expression. She seemed angry that she had spent thousands of dollars to be smuggled to the United States from Honduras and that this man had screwed up her asylum plea.

They admitted that their goal in claiming asylum was to benefit from "catch and release" and get jobs in the United States. Their coyote had advised them that presenting themselves as a family unit would make it easier to achieve that goal.

Normally, I would not make a statement during guilty pleas, but public defenders accepted that a prosecutor might make a statement if a case was particularly unusual or egregious. This was one of those cases. I argued for 180 days in prison for the woman. For the man, without requesting a specific number of days in prison, I asked the judge for a sentence that would both achieve justice while also taking into account that he had voluntarily come forward to admit that the children were not his.

Judge Song chastised the defendants for perverting the U.S. asylum system and giving it a bad name. She was just getting started when the woman's lawyer exclaimed, "She's fainting!" As the female defendant slumped over, the lawyer grabbed her and helped her into a chair. "She's seizing!" As a trained EMT, I could tell she wasn't seizing. I also was skeptical that she had actually fainted. Judge Song appeared skeptical, as well, but she postponed sentencing until the woman could have a medical evaluation.

Back in court a few days later, Judge Song handed down the sentences. The man received thirty days and the woman received ninety days.

After sentencing, Judge Song asked the lawyers if we knew what had happened to the children. Sadly, that wasn't our department.

■ ■ ■

President Trump wants to bar immigrants from seeking asylum after they've entered the United States illegally, and he wants to require asylum seekers to wait in Mexico while their cases are pending.

I believe these measures would go a long way toward fixing our broken system, though both face serious challenges in federal court.

Ultimately, a president cannot fix our immigration problems alone. It is incumbent upon Congress to pass these and other policies into law so that our asylum system can function as intended—as a life-saving option of last resort for those experiencing persecution and not as a backdoor for economic migrants.

CHAPTER 12

THEY COME FROM UNEXPECTED PLACES

Many Americans have preconceived notions about illegal immigrants—that they're poor, they speak Spanish, and they come from Latin America. In most cases I prosecuted, this stereotype was correct. But I also saw many illegal immigrants who did not fit this mold. While 95 percent of the cases I handled involved Spanish speakers from Latin America, in my six months in Laredo, I prosecuted illegal aliens from every continent except Antarctica.

One thing that surprised me was the number of people who came from Spanish-speaking countries but who did not speak Spanish. Instead, they spoke indigenous languages from Guatemala, Ecuador, and Mexico—including languages I had never heard of, such as Mam, Meta, Q'eqchi', K'iche', and others.

When the public defenders found defendants who spoke neither English nor Spanish, they notified the court and the prosecutors, and we would reset their court appearances for a later date when a translator would be available.

Many of the indigenous people we prosecuted were illiterate, so the judge would use Google Translate and a "text to talk" program to inform the defendants of their rights and the movement of their court date not only in writing, but also verbally. Listening to a computer read aloud to a defendant was slow and maddening, especially when it had to be done repeatedly.

Sometimes it would take a week or more to find an available certified translator. In that time, the defendants were held in the detention area. With just two exceptions, every indigenous-language speaker we processed was sentenced to "time served" because it was a first offense and they were the least likely of all illegal immigrants to reoffend, perhaps because they couldn't afford more smuggling fees. Most were "one and done" after getting caught.

I do remember the case of one repeat offender who was from Guatemala and spoke an indigenous language. He had been arrested twice before for trying to enter the country illegally and was charged with misdemeanors. Both times, though, the charges had been dismissed. Judge Song took a very dim view of this third offense and correctly surmised that both prior dismissals had been because the courts had been unable to locate an interpreter. She said to him, "You took advantage of that and kept trying to come here because you weren't being punished." Much to my surprise—and to the surprise of the defense attorney who could not jump in fast enough to stop his client from talking—the defendant confirmed this, adding that he was not a bad guy. Nonetheless, because he had no prior record of actual convictions—even though he had been caught three times—he received only time served.

■ ■ ■

Indigenous-language translators did not operate contemporaneously like the Spanish translators did. Instead, everyone who spoke in court had to stop every sentence or two so that what they said could be translated, which meant that everything was said twice. The translator spoke over a phone with the defendant, and inevitably not only was there the occasional dropped call or poor reception, but indigenous languages often have many dialects. So if the verbal inflections weren't just right, the translator and the defendant might not understand each other.

If the difficulties of translation weren't enough, most of the indigenous people simply could not understand our judicial process and did or said things that slowed it down further. For instance, instead of answering yes or no to the litany of questions the judge was required to ask, they would sometimes say things like "I want to go home" or "I want to go home and will not come back"—not just to the first question, but over and over again. A process that would have taken thirty minutes with a group of forty Spanish-speaking defendants could take as long as two and a half hours with a single indigenous defendant.

■ ■ ■

In one case, we had a woman in her twenties who was the only other indigenous repeat offender whom I prosecuted. Her husband was already in the country illegally and working at a restaurant, and she wanted to join him. She had been convicted of illegal entry and deported just a few months earlier.

Judge Song asked the defendant for her name. "Nothing," she said. The judge, thinking there was a mistranslation, repeated the question. The woman replied, "Nothing."

"What do you mean when you say 'nothing'?"

"I have nothing to say."

The judge pressed on and asked more questions, but the defendant replied repeatedly, "Nothing."

Judge Song called a recess so the woman could consult with her public defender. This, of course, was code to the defense attorney to set the woman straight. For the public defender to speak with the woman using the translator on the telephone, I had to go wait in the hall in order to maintain attorney-client privilege. On my way out, I went up to the public defender and said, "Look, I'm not trying to be an asshole here, but you can tell her if she doesn't cooperate, I'll ask the judge to hold her in contempt." While this may sound harsh, I was actually doing the defense attorney a favor, equipping him with a real-world consequence he could use to get his client to cooperate.

After thirty minutes, I reentered the courtroom, we resumed, and things went smoothly from there. Afterward, I asked the defense attorney what had been going on. He told me she wasn't trying to be uncooperative; she was simply too scared to think straight. Because I was involved in it every day, I sometimes forgot how intimidating the process could be.

■ ■ ■

One thing I never lost sight of was just how expensive it was to process guilty pleas for non-Spanish speakers. For example, one day we had a single reset hearing for a Mam language speaker scheduled for one thirty in the afternoon. However, the public defender asked to spend fifty minutes with the translator and his client to explain the process. Once we started, it took another seventy-five minutes to get through the guilty plea. At that point, the courtroom was staffed with a judge, two clerks, four U.S. Marshals, a Border Patrol agent, one Special Assistant U.S. Attorney (me), a public defender, and a translator. That's eleven people—all funded by U.S. taxpayers—present in court for a single guilty plea. Furthermore, I suspected there were two private security guards out of view who were contracted by the government to transport the defendant between the detention center and court.

All these resources were provided by our government—by our tax dollars—to deal with a person who wasn't even supposed to be here in the first place. That's money that otherwise could have gone toward better schools, drug treatment programs, and other much-needed services that would benefit U.S. citizens.

Bangladeshi Immigrants

Aside from the indigenous language speakers, the other large population of non-Spanish speakers we prosecuted was from Bangladesh. It struck me as odd that so many people from Bangladesh were trying to enter the United States illegally near Laredo. Each week, we processed between one and fifteen Bangladeshi defendants. From the interviews in their A-Files, I gleaned that their smuggling fees were the highest, between eighteen thousand and twenty-eight thousand dollars. Bangladesh was also the only country from which 100 percent of the illegal immigrants I prosecuted were men and 100 percent requested asylum.

The illegal immigrants from Bangladesh proved to be the most difficult group of all for a number of reasons. For starters, they all pretended that they didn't speak English, even though most of them spoke excellent English and didn't even need a translator. They still asked for one anyway. One time, a court clerk said in English to a group of Bangladeshi defendants, "Please raise your right hands so you can be placed under oath," and before the translator had a chance to say anything, nearly all of the Bangladeshi defendants had raised their right hands. A few of them quickly caught themselves and lowered their hands.

All Bangladeshi defendants requested asylum—and indeed had been coached by their coyotes that pretending not to understand English would make their asylum claims more credible (which is not true). For them, Plan A was to sneak into the United States illegally. Plan B, if they were caught, was to claim asylum and stay in the country through the system of "catch and release." None of the Bangladeshi defendants I saw was even remotely qualified for asylum. When asked why they were fearful of returning home, they would give generic, vague answers such as, "Bad people want to hurt me."

The Bangladeshis had a couple of odd traits. First, I noticed that they kept staring at me, the U.S. Marshalls, and Border Patrol agents. I asked a Border Patrol agent about this, and he said Bangladeshi defendants had a thing about asserting their dominance by making others look away. I thought he was joking, but he was serious. Over time I discovered that he was right. It was pretty weird—the defendants, in their orange jumpsuits and chains, trying to engage me, the clerks, and law enforcement officials in staring contests.

I also figured out how to win these contests quickly. If I saw a defendant staring at me, I'd walk up to a law enforcement official, point at the defendant, and quietly say a few words. That worked like a charm—no more staring. Another issue I had with the Bangladeshi defendants was their misogyny. They often were very disrespectful to female guards and Border Patrol agents. If they couldn't ignore them, they would shout at them. They didn't involve them in their staring contests, but they would yell because they thought women had no right to look at *them*. When the Bangladeshis were in front of Judge Song, they strenuously avoided making eye contact with her and were obviously embarrassed that a woman was presiding over them.

Sometimes I wondered why people in favor of open borders don't consider that other people groups have different cultures. Many Americans like to pretend that our values—such as freedom of speech and religion, limited government, equal protection, and due process—are universal. But that's simply not true. Some cultures are misogynistic. In some cultures, having the wrong religion can get you killed. In some cultures, the ideas of due process and limited government are a joke. With a system of legal immigration, we can at least keep immigration at a level where it is easier to assimilate newcomers and where we can design our immigration policies in the national interest. But massive illegal immigration subverts all of that and breeds contempt for our foundational value of the rule of law.

CHAPTER 13

CRIMINAL INFLOW: THE "BAD HOMBRES"

Reading over the defendants' criminal histories sometimes made my blood boil. Every day, I saw people trying to enter the United States illegally who had convictions for serious crimes such as murder, child molestation, and drug trafficking.

People who enter our country illegally have broken the law; many of them will not respect the law once they are here.

Granted, most illegal aliens don't come to the United States in order to commit crimes; they come here to work and to be with their families. Nevertheless, anyone reviewing the illegal aliens' records will find that an alarming number of them have criminal records. In fact, the reason many cross the border illegally is because they have criminal records, which disqualify them from entering the country legally. A very large number had at some point previously lived in the United States legally but had been deported after convictions for serious crimes.

Every morning in court, I had access to the criminal records of the people entering the United States illegally. On nine random days, I copied the information I had available and crunched the data to see how many of the illegal aliens had criminal convictions.

Here is one sample day in court from November 23, 2018:

Total in Group 1	43
Total in Group 2	74
Sum total	117
Previously deported (no other crimes)	35
Convicted of illegal entry or reentry (no other crimes)	18
Serious criminal history	19

Or, in other words, 16 percent of the defendants that day had serious criminal histories—and that doesn't tell the full story, because I discounted minor crimes like traffic offenses. Some had multiple convictions for their crimes, and some were sentenced to longer than usual prison time (indicating that the circumstances of the crimes were particularly egregious).

Here is what another day in court looked like on October 29, 2018:

Total in Group 1	56
Total in Group 2	74
Sum total	130
Previously deported (no other crimes)	34
Convicted of illegal entry or reentry (no other crimes)	16
Serious criminal history	18

For those convicted of serious crimes, most were convicted of DUIs, assault, or battery.

In total, here's what I found:

Total days sampled	9
Total in Group 1	299
Total in Group 2	357
Sum total	656
Previously deported (no other crimes)	142
Convicted of illegal entry or reentry (no other crimes)	91
Non-serious traffic crimes	30
DUI	46
Serious criminal history	94
Violence	27

In other words, including immigration and traffic crimes, a third of the illegal immigrants we processed had a criminal record. Fourteen percent had serious criminal records. About half of that had a record of drunk driving, which amounted to 7 percent of the illegal aliens we prosecuted. What is not being calculated or shown is the number of non-criminal traffic offenses, such as tickets for speeding or not stopping at stop signs, because those did not appear in any background checks or records I had on the defendants. The traffic crimes I did see but did not consider to be serious were misdemeanors such as driving without a license. To be clear, my numbers are not based on criminal records; they are based on actual criminal convictions. There is an important difference: any person charged with a crime will have a criminal record. Roughly one in three Americans has a criminal record and was at some point charged with a crime. However, not every person charged with a crime gets convicted. If a person is charged with a crime and that offense is later dismissed or the person is found "not guilty" at trial, that person still has a criminal record.

Based on my numbers, one in three illegal immigrants has been convicted of a crime while roughly one in three U.S. citizens has a "criminal record." To me, this indicates that per capita, illegal immigrants are committing more crimes than U.S. citizens. In contrast, legal immigrants are less likely to commit a crime than U.S. citizens or illegal immigrants.

Looking at the data, I found myself asking why so many people entering the United States illegally have criminal records. There are a couple reasons for it, one of which is practical and one of which is cultural.

The practical reason that so many illegal immigrants have criminal records is that many of them previously lived in the United States, were deported because they committed crimes, and are now trying to get back into the country to reunite with the families they left behind. I can appreciate that the love for family is very powerful. If there is less than a one-in-three chance of getting caught, who wouldn't try to return to the United States to see his spouse and children?

Another reason for the relatively high number of criminal records among illegal immigrants is that many of them, for cultural reasons, do not have the same respect for the rule of law and property rights that Americans have. For most U.S. citizens, there is a deeply ingrained reverence for the rule of law and individual property rights. It is part of our historical, political, and legal heritage that we are a self-governing, law-abiding people whose fundamental principles are grounded in the English common law tradition of liberty, due process, and personal responsibility. We believe our system has legitimacy, so we follow its rules. Americans can disagree over particular laws, but typically we abide by them—like when we stop and wait at red lights late at night when there are no other cars around. I've been in many other countries where no one does that!

Not all cultures have this same respect for the rule of law. They do not necessarily believe that the laws are legitimate—and in some corrupt and incompetent countries, they aren't. Many illegal immigrants come from cultures were corruption is an ordinary and expected fact of life. For instance, I was surprised when I was student in Brazil that my Brazilian classmates assumed that people in public office would naturally use their positions to benefit themselves and their families. They weren't fazed when the president of the university used school funds to take me and other American students to a restaurant his family owned. Although they recognized it as "corrupt," they didn't recognize it as "wrong" or "immoral." On a more mundane level, I found that taxi drivers in Mexico—at least the ones I rode with and saw—ignored red lights if there were no other cars around; in fact, they wouldn't even slow down. They had no respect for traffic laws; it was all about what you could get away with.

In examining the criminal backgrounds of the illegal aliens we processed, I was very troubled by the many prior convictions for domestic violence—cases of men battering women and vice versa. As a criminal defense attorney in Virginia, a disproportionate number of my clients in such cases are noncitizens. And unlike U.S. citizens, my foreign clients and their victims are frequently shocked that the United States government would intervene in what they call nothing more than a minor and personal "family dispute." When they tell me that a woman with a black eye or a man with a scratched face is not a big deal in their culture, I have to tell them that in the United States it is a very big deal and is totally unacceptable.

■ ■ ■

Some people see illegal immigration as a victimless crime, probably because most illegal aliens simply come here to work. But from my time on the border, I came to appreciate that there are far more victims than people realize. Illegal immigration enriches the drug cartels along the border—and that creates plenty of victims, as evidenced by the numerous mass graves regularly uncovered in Mexico. Some of the illegal immigrants' criminal records were truly appalling, and they posed a direct threat to Americans as potential reoffenders. One man I prosecuted for illegal reentry was a former lawyer and green card holder who previously had been deported after a lengthy prison sentence for raping his twelve-year-old niece. Another was a gang member covered in tattoos who smiled proudly after Judge Song noted in his record that he had kicked a man nearly to death.

Illegal immigration also has economic consequences for lower-class American workers. They endure the downward pressure on wages that comes from an inflated labor force and risk being displaced from their jobs by lower-priced illegal immigrants. Although we are frequently told that illegal aliens are only taking jobs that Americans won't do, on the border I saw that wasn't true. When illegal aliens were interviewed after being apprehended, they would be asked about where they were headed and the jobs they were going to take. Many planned on taking jobs that otherwise would be taken by Americans—especially poor, young, minority Americans (such as at fast food restaurants).

Another neglected victim of illegal immigration is the American taxpayer. Many of the illegal aliens stated during their interviews or in court that they were here to take advantage of the American welfare system and other taxpayer-funded services. Of course, they didn't phrase it that way, but instead would say, "I want to bring my children here so they can go to American schools"—which are paid for by local property taxes that illegal aliens do not pay (because few own homes, and they often pay rent under the table).

■ ■ ■

In many cases, illegal immigrants were placed in Group 1 because they did not have any criminal history in the United States. Although we didn't know it at the time, some of those illegal immigrants did have serious criminal records in their countries of origin. Some illegal immigrants were fleeing legal trouble back home. In one instance, a man entered an asylum claim, citing a fear of government persecution if he returned home. After doing some digging, we discovered this was because he was wanted for attempted murder!

In another case, we obtained the criminal record of an illegal alien from El Salvador. He had been a gang member and served twenty-one years in prison for murder. After serving his sentence, he fled to seek asylum in the United States because rival gang members were out to kill him.

■ ■ ■

The records I saw only listed criminal convictions—not the original criminal charges, which could be deceptive—because convictions are often plea-bargained down from more serious charges. I had one case where an illegal immigrant's criminal record showed a conviction for aggravated assault. It turned out that this was part of a plea bargain because his original charge had been for manslaughter. He had served 177 days in prison for assault, after which he was deported. Then he illegally reentered the United States.

Because illegal immigrants convicted of crimes are generally deported, they often receive lenient sentences, even by the standards of plea bargains. The logic is this: Why spend money incarcerating someone who's going to be deported anyway? As a criminal defense attorney, I have argued this point myself to win less jail time for my clients in plea bargains. But however much economic sense it makes, it doesn't seem fair that American citizens receive harsher jail sentences than illegal aliens do.

■ ■ ■

Many of the illegal aliens engaged in criminal activity were also drug addicts, and this created problems in the courtroom because they would often show withdrawal symptoms. I experienced this my first time running the docket when an illegal immigrant on our list didn't show up in court. I panicked, wondering if we had missed something. But Judge Kazen let us know that there had been a "medical issue." A U.S. Marshal later came up to me and whispered, "Heroin withdrawal." This happened multiple times after that, usually because of withdrawal symptoms from opioids or alcohol.

■ ■ ■

One of my many complaints about the mainstream media's coverage of illegal immigration is that it often ignores the fact that large numbers of illegal aliens are dangerous criminals.

In particular, I remember the story of college student Mollie Tibbetts, who went out for a jog in July 2018 and never came back. This happened shortly after I got to the border, and Mollie Tibbetts's disappearance was a national sensation; it became an even bigger story after the police found her corpse. But the media lost interest once it was discovered that her alleged killer was an illegal alien. Now, instead of a news story, it became a political issue as politicians jumped onto the case. Republicans cited the alleged murder as another reason for demanding stricter enforcement of our border laws. Democrats like Senator Elizabeth Warren tried to assert that the real issue wasn't illegal immigrant crime, but was the administration's policies at the border, such as "family separation"—as if Mollie Tibbetts hadn't been separated from her family for forever.

For me, it is a simple matter of law and common sense. According to the General Accounting Office, in five states alone—Arizona, California, New York, Texas, and Florida—5,400 illegal aliens were in prison for homicide-related offenses. That is 5,400 people who should not have been in this country in the first place. If politicians are serious about saving lives, they need to be serious about enforcing our borders and deporting dangerous illegal aliens.

CHAPTER 14

DRUGS, FIREARMS, AND DISEASES

N o book about the southern border would be complete without a discussion of drugs, firearms, and diseases—which are all transported across the border. The cartels' illegal cross-border drug trade, for example, is estimated to have revenues between nineteen billion and twenty-nine billion dollars a year. The Mexican drug cartels weren't always as big and powerful as they are today. Through the 1980s, they mostly focused on marijuana, while more dangerous and lucrative drugs, such as cocaine, were mostly produced and trafficked by the Colombian cartels. But the Colombian drug wars have done major damage to the cartels there and created an opening for the Mexican cartels, given that U.S. demand remains strong. At the same time, a new and younger generation has risen to command the Mexican cartels—and these leaders lack the few moral scruples that prevented their predecessors from trafficking in hard drugs.

The Mexican cartels started getting into cocaine, meth, heroin, and other drugs in the 1990s. This increased their wealth and power—and sparked gang wars between rival cartels competing for market share.

The fuel for the drug wars of Central and South America is the insatiable demand in the United States for illegal drugs. We prosecuted at least one person charged with smuggling drugs into the United States almost every day I was in Laredo. There were so many drugs coming across the border that we spoke about the quantities in kilograms. In Virginia, most drug distribution cases I've handled could be measured in grams or ounces. And in Virginia, most drugs are "watered down" with additives to increase their mass, whereas most of the drugs seized at the border were 99 percent pure.

In Laredo, most cases of drug smuggling involved marijuana, cocaine, heroin, meth, and fentanyl (a synthetic opioid that has become popular among those addicted to heroin or pain pills). In my first case in Laredo involving fentanyl, the defendant was charged with smuggling 4.2 kilograms of the drug (he traveled by taxi with the drug in a bag). According to CNN, 0.25 milligrams is all it takes to cause an overdose death, while Drug Enforcement Administration (DEA) sources put the figure at 2 milligrams. Using the more conservative DEA estimate, the 4.2 kilograms that the woman was trying to smuggle into the United States would be enough to kill 2.1 million people!

■ ■ ■

Most of the border consists of private ranches—often isolated with little access to public roads—that provide a good opportunity for smugglers to avoid detection. One of the largest drug seizures I saw when I was in Laredo was of more than three hundred kilograms of marijuana that was brought across the Rio Grande by boat and smuggled through a private ranch.

In other cases, illegal aliens told us in court that prior to crossing the border, the cartels had packed them with drugs. Some told us they had protested, at least initially, and were beaten or threatened with execution.

One day, we had a case involving two aliens who said they had been forced to smuggle drugs into the United States. They claimed to have been driving in Mexico when they were forced off the road by armed gunmen. The gunmen had shown them pictures of their families, saying they were at risk if they didn't cooperate, and placed drugs in their vehicles. The gunmen ordered them to drive across the border to a specified location. After court, I asked their public defender if he believed their story. He shrugged and said, "Wouldn't be the first time." (This was a standard line for public defenders who never really knew if their clients were being truthful.)

Most of the drugs we seized were discovered at lawful ports of entry. At these checkpoints, there are K-9s and ICE officers trained to look for signs of drug trafficking. The dogs are some of the best tools we have, but even they are not entirely reliable—a change in wind patterns, or even a dog's mood on a given day, could cause the dog to fail to signal for the presence of drugs.

Also, smugglers are very creative and are constantly testing new methods for hiding drugs as they come through legal ports of entry. Sometimes, they would add compartments to their vehicles, such as under the driver's seat carpet, inside the tires (we prosecuted one man who had been caught with nearly thirty-six kilograms of cocaine hidden in his tires), affixed to the car battery, or sewn into the seats. Well-trained and perceptive Border Patrol agents were experts at detecting such alterations.

■ ■ ■

The cartels recruit and pay poor Mexicans and Americans to do dangerous smuggling jobs for them. Even in big busts that made the headlines, the smugglers were almost always minor figures; the cartel members are too smart to take those risks themselves. One woman we prosecuted was a United States citizen—a single mother with no criminal history who had fallen on hard economic times and was in danger of losing her home. She accepted two thousand dollars to drive about eighteen kilograms of meth across the border. She was sentenced to eight years in federal prison. By comparison, if she had instead driven eighteen illegal aliens through an interior checkpoint, the cartels would have paid her eighteen thousand dollars, and if caught, she would have likely only received between eighteen and thirty-six months in prison.

In another case, we prosecuted two people who had been busted at a border checkpoint with more than twenty-two kilograms of meth and more than nine kilograms of cocaine. The driver was paid eight thousand dollars and brought a friend who was promised a small cut—between one thousand and fifteen hundred dollars—to go along (perhaps he thought the passenger would make him look less suspicious). The friend said she knew he was smuggling something illegal, but she didn't know what. I wondered if she knew how much he was getting paid.

■ ■ ■

U.S. law enforcement officers are quick to notice trends in how drugs are smuggled. There were a few weeks when car tires were the hiding place of choice; then there were a few weeks when it was inside car seats. And so on. These trends might have been driven in part by a cartel recruitment tactic. The cartels bought vehicles for the smugglers, who were allowed to keep them—and one smuggler's success in hiding drugs in tires (or elsewhere) could inspire others. The cars were typically cheap models, like Nissan Versas, and were often painted white.

■ ■ ■

Drug traffickers take advantage of any opportunity for getting drugs into the United States, no matter how deranged or immoral. One program they exploited was humanitarian parole. This is when people are admitted into the United States temporarily for humanitarian reasons, such as the funeral of a family member or to visit a sick relative. In August, we processed a woman who had been arrested with twenty kilograms of cocaine who had been trying to enter the United States on humanitarian parole to visit her niece in the hospital. She only got caught because the Border Patrol agent at the checkpoint remembered her using the same exact pretense weeks prior.

A surprising number of people walking across the bridge from Mexico into the United States were drug smugglers with drugs strapped to their torsos, stuffed into hidden pockets, concealed in their shoes, or even stuck up their rectums (a Border Patrol agent told us these smugglers were easy to spot because they walked funny).

In reviewing my court notes, I found this entry: "Normal day in court. One person had 15.7kg of heroine, 7.4kg of fentanyl, and 59.28kg of meth." We had a lot of days like that.

■ ■ ■

Given how lucrative the drug trade is, there are ample opportunities for the people we entrust with guarding the border to become corrupted. It's a major embarrassment for our country whenever representatives of U.S. Customs and Border Protection are caught being paid to look the other way.

Fortunately, there were no cases of this in my sector while I was in Laredo. The worst case I saw of a similar crime involved a U.S. National Guard soldier whose family had fallen onto hard financial times. He had access to the room where confiscated drugs were stored and had swiped a package of 1.5 kilograms of meth. His grand plan, he confessed, was to sell the meth for ten thousand dollars. But he decided to try it first, and because he had never used meth before and didn't know what he was doing, he overdosed and ended up in the hospital with barely functioning kidneys.

Firearms

When people think of smuggling at the border, they usually imagine contraband moving in one direction: northward, from Mexico to the United States. But there is also a robust smuggling operation going southward, exporting firearms from the United States to Mexico. In fact, Mexico's drug wars would not be possible without the firearms and ammunition supplied by sources in the United States.

While the Second Amendment of the Constitution guarantees U.S. citizens the right to bear arms, no such right exists in Mexico. There, the mere possession of a firearm can result in a two-year prison sentence. All along the border there are signs warning Americans not to bring their firearms into Mexico.

While I was shadowing U.S. Customs and Border Protection officials at a checkpoint one day, we witnessed something odd: In a span of thirty minutes, an old vehicle entered the United States, returned to Mexico, and then reentered the United States. The driver was directed to pull over for questioning. He said he had been rock climbing in Mexico and explained that his return to Mexico and reentry back into the United States was because he realized he'd forgotten something back in Mexico. The equipment in his vehicle supported his story of being a rock climber. Hidden in his vehicle, buried under a stack of gear, was a pistol and a small amount of marijuana. The pistol presented a serious legal problem, while the quantity of marijuana was too small to warrant charges.

Already, the driver had committed a crime by failing to declare a firearm when he crossed the border.

"Why didn't you declare it?" the Border Patrol agent asked him.

"I'm a veteran, so I earned the right," he responded.

"Yeah, well, you could spend two years in a Mexican prison for that."

"Yeah, whatever; I'm not scared."

We decided to let him go—but before driving off, he had the audacity to ask if he could get his marijuana back. (The answer was no.)

■ ■ ■

Gun smuggling relies on U.S. citizens with clean records who purchase firearms and ammunition in the United States and transfer them to contacts in the cartels for between $100 and $250 per weapon. The cartels have smuggling routes, networks, and methods for getting the weapons and ammunition into Mexico. One day in court, we processed a woman who had been part of a gun-smuggling ring. The ring smuggled parts to modify semi-automatic weapons into automatic weapons; the ring also smuggled magazines for AK-47 assault rifles. Another day in court, we had a defendant charged with conspiracy for trying to transport 1,800 rounds of ammunition in her car trunk to Mexico. The way I viewed it, that was 1,800 potential murder victims.

One of the weirdest bond hearings I litigated was for a man accused of modifying firearms in the United States and selling them in Mexico. He was a convicted felon and had no right to even touch a firearm. His home had been raided, and numerous firearms were found in a safe. The man's wife insisted the firearms belonged to her, not to her husband. But the story hit a snag: the wife could not remember the combination to the safe, and in the presence of law enforcement, her husband helpfully volunteered that information.

■ ■ ■

One day, I struck up a conversation with a Border Patrol agent who had worked in intelligence. I asked him about the Mexican hitmen who were prime users of the guns smuggled from the United States to Mexico.

I learned from the agent that the going rate for a hit in Nuevo Laredo was three thousand dollars. I thought that seemed like a frighteningly low value for a human life. The agent pointed out that for the hitmen, there was a very low chance of being caught, and if they carried out a few hits per month, they could live quite well in Mexico.

Diseases

Before my trip to Laredo, I didn't look after my health as well as I should have and relied on my wife to remind me of things like flu shots or regular checkups. But what I saw at the border provided a strong motivation for me to start taking the initiative to stay clean and healthy. I developed a habit of aggressively washing my hands whenever I exited the courtroom, and I got my annual flu shot the day it became available. I also checked to make sure I was up to date on all my vaccinations.

The reason for this, of course, was that I saw firsthand the diseases and illnesses that illegal aliens were bringing with them into our country. There were many instances where the immigrants that we were processing had visible skin diseases or needed to have their hearings postponed so they could be treated for parasites.

Many of the illegal aliens were brought into court wearing surgical scrubs and masks. The Bangladeshi immigrants were the sickliest and often came to court with severe coughs. One day in court, there were eight Bangladeshi defendants lined up in front of Judge Kazen; four of them were wearing surgical masks and coughing incessantly. According to the World Health Organization, tuberculosis is a major problem in Bangladesh. It certainly seemed to be present among those who tried to cross our southern border.

Another day in court, there were only men present. Although more than 90 percent of illegal immigrants were men, on a normal day there would always be at least a few women present in court. I noticed on my sheet that every woman who had been scheduled to be sentenced that morning had been given a medical reset. I asked the U.S. Marshals about this, and they told me it was because the women's area of the detention center was under quarantine because of a chickenpox outbreak. This is one of many childhood diseases—along with measles, mumps, and others—that have been all but eliminated in the United States through vaccinations but are still rife south of the border. It was lucky that we had caught the illegal alien with chickenpox before she was able to enter the country and potentially infect children too young to be vaccinated or people who chose not to get vaccinated. But this is a small comfort, given that only 30 percent of illegal aliens are caught.

It's a plain fact: an unsecured border with Mexico represents a major health hazard for the people of the United States.

CHAPTER 15

SUPPORTING THE BORDER PATROL

I came away from Laredo with a deep admiration for the Border Patrol. I interacted with agents on a daily basis and found them to be extremely professional and passionate about defending our country. These agents saw firsthand the dangers at the southern border and were patriots determined to defend the land they loved. Many of them had previously served in the military, especially the Marine Corps. They took great pride in their work—not just in protecting the country, but also in caring for and (in some cases) saving the lives of the illegal immigrants they caught crossing the border. Border Patrol agents have a very hard job, and unfortunately, despite all of their great work, morale among Border Patrol agents was very low—in part because of the endless attacks against them from the media and radical leftist politicians.

The left often accuses federal law enforcement officials at the border of racism, which is ludicrous. The vast majority of Border Patrol agents I met were Hispanic. Overall, 52 percent of Border Patrol agents are Hispanic—a statistic you're not likely to hear on CNN or MSNBC.

The Border Patrol agents I met were not motivated by racism or xenophobia. They were law enforcement officers dedicated to upholding the law of the land as enacted through our democratic process. Of course, I am not a mind reader, but I never witnessed anyone say or do anything that was remotely racist. Like all members of law enforcement, their job is to enforce the law as it currently is, regardless of whether they—or the public—agree or disagree with it.

This isn't to say that Border Patrol doesn't have problems. For one thing, of the two thousand agents in my sector, we had two charged for horrific murders that shocked the tight-knit Border Patrol community. One of the agents, Juan David Ortiz, had been with the Border Patrol for a decade when he was charged with killing four women—all of whom had worked as prostitutes. The other agent, Ronald Anthony Burgos-Aviles, was charged with killing his secret lover and their one-year-old son. The convictions left the Border Patrol stunned and were a major blow to the morale of the force. It was hard for the agents to believe that they had such monsters in their midst. Still, these were terrible, isolated incidents.

A broader problem involves training. The Border Patrol is a paramilitary force that learns skills that traditional law enforcement officers do not learn, such as how to track people through the Texas brush. However, this training comes at the expense of learning other rules and procedures familiar to local police. For example, if Border Patrol agents suspected that a vehicle was transporting illegal aliens, they would often follow the car and wait for the driver to commit a traffic violation so they could pull it over. Unfortunately, because Border Patrol agents weren't as well-versed in traffic laws as they should have been, there were instances where they pulled over vehicles for behaviors that were not illegal. We had to drop one case against a human trafficker because the Border Patrol agent had mistakenly believed the smuggler's vehicle had made an illegal turn. In another case, I had to dismiss charges against human smugglers when a federal judge ruled that the Border Patrol agent did not have enough evidence of human trafficking to support the stop (which had led to the discovery of four concealed illegal aliens).

Another problem is a lack of trial experience. More so than in state courts, nearly every case in federal courts results in the defendant pleading guilty. Because of this, we had law enforcement officers who had been on the force for more than a decade without ever testifying at a trial. When I did have cases that looked like they might go to trial, I had to teach the basic fundamentals of testifying to the agents involved.

A third problem, which is also partly the result of the lack of trial experience, is sloppy evidence collection. Because of the expectation that defendants would just enter guilty pleas, there were some instances where Border Patrol agents were not as diligent or thorough as they should have been in gathering and preserving evidence. For example, I had what seemed like an easy case against a woman who had been arrested for human smuggling. She crossed the border with an illegal immigrant she intended to employ as her domestic servant. But I ended up having to dismiss the charge because law enforcement officers had failed to acquire and preserve text messages in a timely manner.

Border Patrol agents have challenges that other federal law enforcement officials don't have. For instance, federal law enforcement investigations into public corruption, organized crime, white-collar crime, and so forth are generally done at a steady pace that allows time for the legal review of any proposed methods, strategies, warrants, and evidence collection. At the border, things happen much more rapidly and require significant improvisation. In fact, the volume and pace are overwhelming, which means that there aren't enough resources, time, or manpower to put the care and attention into a single case as there would be in a federal investigation elsewhere.

Based on my experiences from my time in Laredo, I'd say that we clearly need more Border Patrol officers. They also need more resources. And Congress needs to get serious about restoring the integrity of our southern border. It is Congress, not the Border Patrol, that deserves to be criticized. It is Congress that—sometimes openly—makes a mockery of its own laws by siding, apparently for political reasons, with illegal immigrants against the Border Patrol.

It was clear to this prosecutor that the criminals who exhaust our overwhelmed Border Patrol agents directly threaten the safety and security of our country.

CHAPTER 16

PUBLIC DEFENDERS AND THE U.S. JUSTICE DEPARTMENT

In Laredo, public defenders far outnumber prosecutors—a situation that is very different from Virginia, where there's a shortage of public defenders because of low pay and overwhelming caseloads. At the border, the public defenders were better paid and had more experience than our relatively young U.S. Attorney's Office prosecutors, and we suffered from far higher turnover. Many of the public defenders had been state or federal prosecutors before switching to defense.

Among the general public, court-appointed lawyers do not have a good reputation, but the public defenders I worked with in Laredo were outstanding attorneys who did incredible work for their clients. Defendants were lucky to receive such high-quality legal representation from lawyers who genuinely cared about them and their cases.

In instances where the Federal Public Defender's Office had a conflict, such as when there were multiple defendants who might have reason to testify against one another, a local attorney in private practice would be appointed as defense counsel. This often occurred when public defenders were representing illegal immigrants who planned to testify against their smuggler. In these cases, the smuggler would be assigned a private attorney who was a member of the Criminal Justice Association, which we referred to as the "CJA list." In Laredo, these were extremely experienced attorneys, many of whom had been practicing longer than I'd been alive. To get on the CJA list, attorneys had to be vetted by judges who held them to a very high standard. Getting to prosecute cases against defendants represented by such experienced attorneys was an invaluable learning experience for me.

Not only was it an honor to be on the CJA list, but it could also be quite lucrative. These lawyers billed the court $148 per hour for federal work, and this included the time they spent sitting around waiting for their cases to be called. By contrast, in state court in Virginia, private attorneys appointed to cases are capped at $120 for misdemeanors and $445 for most felonies. At this low rate—and given the amount of time they put into their cases—court-appointed attorneys in Virginia sometimes work below minimum wage.

■ ■ ■

In Laredo, my job as a prosecutor wasn't to put every single defendant behind bars for as long as possible; it was to do justice. The defense attorney's job was to make sure I followed the rules—including the rules of evidence—and that I respected his client's rights. Even though our justice system is based on an adversarial model, prosecutors and defense attorneys often collaborate on cases to make sure justice is done. There were many instances where public defenders brought issues to my attention that resulted in charges being dismissed. For example, if the public defenders discovered that a defendant was a juvenile, or that the statute of limitations had run out, I would readily agree to dismiss the charges. Because of the overwhelming volume of cases we had, we were practically looking for any reason to dismiss a bad case, which would free us up to dedicate our time to the good ones.

Usually, these situations were pretty clear-cut, but they weren't always. In one case involving human smuggling, the defense attorney filed a motion to suppress—to exclude evidence. He argued that his client's vehicle had been unlawfully pulled over because there was a lack of "reasonable articulable suspicion of unlawful conduct," and therefore anything discovered in the search of the vehicle could not be used as evidence. He and I discussed the situation, and while I thought he had some strong arguments, I didn't think they were winning arguments. The standard for "reasonable suspicion" is very low, and I believed there was enough evidence to meet it. We argued the case before the judge, who ended up ruling that the stop was illegal. As a result, I ultimately had to dismiss the charge after being advised by both the U.S. Attorney's Office in Laredo and our headquarters in Houston that an appeal was unlikely to prevail.

Given the nature of most cases on the border, there usually isn't much question of a defendant's guilt. For instance, if a vehicle is stopped and illegal immigrants are found hiding in the trunk, there is generally no plausible or innocent explanation. Also, although everyone is advised of their right to remain silent, the vast majority of defendants gave full confessions, hoping to be deported as quickly as possible instead of being held in U.S.

detention centers. In addition, because the U.S. Attorney's Office was so overwhelmed and understaffed, we only prosecuted cases that were very strong. This meant the Federal Public Defender's Office had little to work with.

■ ■ ■

I built strong working relationships with the public defenders in Laredo, and although most of the criminal defense attorneys I worked with were outstanding, there were a couple of exceptions—both of which involved privately retained lawyers. While lawyers have to be vetted and hired by the government as prosecutors and public defenders or approved by judges to make the CJA list, any idiot with a law degree can start a private practice as a criminal defense attorney and use slick marketing to attract clients.

I met one such attorney when I was sorting the paperwork for Groups 1 and 2. She approached me and introduced herself as an immigration lawyer who also practiced criminal law. She told me the name of her client, and I could see that he was listed in Group 2 for that morning. She asked me if I would dismiss the charge against him, saying that he had a reason to be in the United States. (Everyone has a reason to be here, but few in court had one that is a legal justification.) I politely but firmly shut her down, pulling up the file and asking, "Did he enter the country illegally?" This was my way of signaling that my view of the case would be based on whether or not her client broke the law, not on his personal immigration needs.

Rather than answering my question, the woman told me her client didn't have any criminal or immigration history. I was surprised to hear this because he was in Group 2, which is specifically reserved for those with previous immigration or criminal offenses. I pointed out this discrepancy, and she responded, "Can I see the charge?" This caused me to wonder whether the woman was even a real lawyer, because lawyers always ask to see "the file," not "the charge."

The Border Patrol agent in court that morning searched for the A-File. While we waited, I consulted my cheat sheet and saw that her client had been deported twice! When I showed this to the lawyer, she said that she believed it was a mistake; it was actually two voluntary returns—not deportations. I kept an open mind because I had seen many previous errors on my cheat sheet. Rather than arguing, I said, "Let's check the file."

When the Border Patrol agent found her client's A-File, he confirmed that her client had two prior deportations. The lawyer didn't look surprised; instead, she told me that someone can have a deportation that's also a voluntary return. I was still pretty inexperienced at the time, but that didn't sound right to me. I took a closer look at my cheat sheet and saw that her client's date of entry was 2008, which indicated that he had entered then and had been here ever since. I showed this to the lawyer, and she responded with a blank smile, seemingly unaware of why I was telling her this. I didn't want to insult her intelligence, so I rephrased my statement, saying, "I think the illegal entry in 2008 might be your better argument."

She still stared dumbly at me, not getting it, so I said, "The statute of limitations is five years."

It took a few seconds for this to register. Finally, she said, "So you'll dismiss it?"

"I'll have to," I replied, getting exasperated at her incompetence. "But first I want to see the file and what statements he made."

As noted, there were often errors on my cheat sheet, and before dismissing charges, I would always check the A-File. In this case, it turned out that "2008" was a typo. In his interview, the woman's client had admitted to entering the country eight days prior to his recent arrest—not in 2008.

This, of course, took the "statute of limitations" defense off the board. At this point, the lawyer told me that she hadn't spoken to her client yet, and she walked away. I was absolutely flabbergasted that a defense attorney would make requests from a prosecutor before even speaking to her client.

Ultimately, her client pleaded guilty to illegal entry. I felt bad for his family because they wasted their money on this idiot.

Prosecutors and the Justice Department

I have enormous respect for my fellow prosecutors in Laredo. They were sharp, talented, hardworking, dedicated to the administration of justice, and deserved the highest praise for doing a tough job extremely well under adverse conditions. We also had a great support staff of paralegals and assistants, and the Assistant United States Attorney-in-Charge was the best boss any attorney could have.

On the other hand, I felt nothing but contempt for the lawyers back in D.C. who were running the Justice Department. Despite all the lip service paid to the importance of securing the border, they left us critically understaffed, forcing each of our prosecutors to handle more than four times the number of cases they would handle at any other U.S. Attorney's Office that wasn't on the border. The lawyers back in D.C. weren't just clueless about how bad the situation on the border was; they were completely uninterested in finding out. I know this because during my six months in Laredo, not once did a top official from the Justice Department visit or check in on us at the site of the second-highest number of illegal border crossings in the nation. As a result, the U.S. prosecutors at the border felt isolated and burdened by a distant bureaucracy that ignored their pressing need for more support.

Mid-level Justice Department attorneys did sometimes come to Laredo when we had a big case, showing up for a couple of court dates and claiming partial credit when we got a conviction. This allowed them to pad their resumes without doing any actual work. For example, in a case handled by one of our top prosecutors, a D.C. lawyer was assigned as a "Trial Advisor" even though he had never done an actual trial!

■ ■ ■

The Justice Department's bureaucracy was difficult and annoying. Whenever I dismissed a felony, I had to fill out a lengthy form explaining why I dismissed the case, instead of spending my time moving on to the next case where I could get a conviction. These forms had to be reviewed and signed by my boss, who had far more important things to do than file memos with bureaucrats in Washington.

In one instance, I had to dismiss charges because I had lost a suppression hearing. With the key evidence suppressed, the government no longer had a case. Instead of spending my time working on a different case, I spent an afternoon writing up a memo about losing the hearing and weighing the pros and cons of an appeal. I had been advised by my boss that because of the way the judge had ruled, we had very little chance of winning on appeal. After the memo was reviewed by my boss, who agreed with it, I was about to go and dismiss the charge before he stopped me. He said that even though he and I both agreed that the charge should be dismissed, I still needed to send it to the head of our appeals division in Houston. I sent it to that person, and she concurred with the AUSA-in-Charge and told me that it would be inadvisable to appeal. Based on what she said, I went ahead and dismissed the charge.

A day or two later, I got a call from someone in Houston about that case. He talked about the next steps and started telling me about some other forms or motions I'd have to file up the chain of command with the Department of Justice. I was so sick of this endless bureaucracy that I politely but firmly cut him off, telling him that I had already dismissed the case. There was a long pause before he told me that I had made a mistake, and before I dismissed the case, Houston needed to draft a memo and have it reviewed by appellate lawyers in Washington, who would then write their own memo to the solicitor general for a final decision. Only then could I dismiss the charges. Although he took a professional and corrective tone with me, I could hear the relief in his voice that my mistake had saved many people a lot of time, research, and memo-drafting for a case that would have been dismissed anyway.

■ ■ ■

Shortly after I arrived in Laredo, Attorney General Jeff Sessions arrived in Houston. I was disappointed, to say the least, that Sessions couldn't be bothered to visit the actual border in person. His "visit" consisted of a video conference with the offices in our district. To my amazement, he chastised us, saying that we weren't doing our jobs because the number of convictions and average sentences had both declined, and he wanted those numbers up. He sounded like someone presiding over a shareholders meeting and complaining that profits were down. Scanning the room, I could tell that my colleagues were as outraged by what Sessions said as I was. We were upset because our job is to do justice—not just convict people—and they weren't giving us enough prosecutors and other resources to get more convictions!

Sessions barely talked about illegal immigration, which surprised me. Based on the tone of the Trump administration, I would have thought that this would be his main focus. Instead, he mostly talked about the illegal drug trade and why he thought that legalizing marijuana would make our problems worse, not better. But all in all, Sessions came across as arrogant and condescending, with little understanding of the work we were doing or the actual situation at the border.

That meeting was one of the greatest disappointments of my deployment. When I had first heard that Jeff Sessions was coming, I thought he would be like a general who comes to the field to inspect the troops and observe the situation. Instead, he remained in the comforts of Houston.

It was hard to regard the Justice Department as much of an ally. It was distant, unhelpful, and much more focused on bureaucratic and federal politics than in getting the job done at the border. If Jeff Sessions was the administration's point-man on border enforcement, it was obvious that we were in trouble. He might talk a harder line than the Obama administration officials, but it was not clear that he had any better grasp of the realities of the crisis on the border.

EPILOGUE

At the end of my deployment to Laredo, I asked myself the same question I had asked myself near the beginning: *What am I doing here?*

I had been full of optimism when I had answered the "urgent" call for special prosecutors at the border. But as I prepared to leave Laredo, I wondered whether I'd accomplished much of anything. I was proud to have served, but the crisis at the border was so big and so overwhelming that any contribution I made felt insignificant.

I support the Trump administration's "zero tolerance" policy for illegal immigration because I believe in enforcing the laws, but I also know that we cannot prosecute our way to a solution. In fact, for the goal of stopping or deterring illegal immigration, most prosecutions are meaningless because the vast majority of defendants are sentenced to "time served" or short jail sentences—and are then deported, free to sneak into our country again. They are highly motivated by money and family to come to the United States, and a little time in jail will not stop them.

So how do we fix the nation's border crisis?

First, we must secure the border. Because we are not securing it, the Mexican drug cartels have filled the power vacuum, and right now they are the ones determining who will enter our country—not the U.S. government. How we go about securing the border should be decided not by faraway politicians and bureaucrats back in D.C. with no expertise in border security, but by the U.S. Border Patrol officials who are actually on the scene and know what they need in each particular sector. The tools they need to secure the border depend on the circumstances of each area. We should absolutely be investing in a combination of walls, cameras, motion detectors, roads, and—above all else—more members of law enforcement. It is important to remember that cameras and walls don't actually arrest anyone—people do. What walls, cameras, and motion detectors do is make it easier for Border Patrol agents to arrive on time to make arrests. We should allow the U.S. Border Patrol in each sector to determine what resources it needs to do its job better—and Congress should provide them.

While I will leave it to the Border Patrol to decide what equipment it needs and where the agency needs it, what is beyond question is that it needs more manpower; the agents do a tremendous job, but they are simply overwhelmed by the massive number of illegal immigrants crossing the border—not to mention the huge influx of drugs—and other law enforcement issues they face every day. Securing the border is step one for stopping illegal immigration—and the Border Patrol is our first line of defense.

Our second line of defense is prosecutions, but the Justice Department has the wrong priorities. Given how many repeat offenders there are, it is obvious that prosecuting and deporting illegal aliens after slap-on-the-wrist prison sentences has a limited deterrent effect. Instead of making a priority of prosecuting border jumpers, the Department of Justice should be focused on prosecuting the employers who hire illegal aliens and the family members who pay the illegal aliens' cartel fees. Reducing the demand for illegal aliens will reduce the supply, and prosecuting those who fund the cartels will help put the human traffickers out of business.

We must also overhaul our broken asylum system. Our asylum system was created to save the lives of people being persecuted, but today it is being abused by illegal immigrants who simply see it as a way to benefit from a policy of "catch and release." The Trump administration has tried to implement reforms, such as barring asylum claims from anyone who tries entering the country illegally first instead of applying for asylum directly at a lawful port of entry. But this commonsensical reform was blocked by activist judges. It's time for Congress to step up, do its job, and pass legislation mandating asylum reform.

Next, we need real consequences—tougher sentences—for those who cross the border illegally. Right now, about half receive sentences of "time served" and half receive fewer than six months in prison. Tougher sentencing is a matter of respect for the rule of law. It is also a matter of justice for American taxpayers and lawful immigrants who followed the rules to enter this country.

■ ■ ■

In December of 2018, after six months on the border, I returned home to Richmond, Virginia. In some ways, life returned to normal. I reopened my law firm and resumed my busy practice as a criminal defense attorney. I also resumed teaching homeland security law at Virginia Commonwealth University (VCU). I utilized my experiences at the border to better teach my students, and I also hope to achieve this goal with the general public by writing this book. The most dramatic change in my life was the birth of my beautiful daughter a little more than nine months after I returned home.

Locally, I have become an (almost) D-List celebrity of sorts, having been invited to speak about my time in Laredo to a number of civic groups. I emphasize to them that securing our southern border should not be a political issue; it is simply a matter of enforcing our laws, something upon which Republicans and Democrats should be able to agree. Until we come together as a nation to defend our southern border, the humanitarian crisis there will only get worse, and the cartels will only grow richer and more dangerous.

AMERICA'S FUTURE IS IN OUR HANDS

You have just read a remarkable and plainspoken eyewitness account of what it's like to serve as a federal prosecutor handling illegal immigration cases on the border in Laredo, Texas. You probably found it eye-opening. I know I did. It's a dramatic snapshot of a national problem.

I'm a native of North Carolina, but after twenty years as an active duty Air Force pilot, serving in combat operations in Grenada, Bosnia, the Persian Gulf, Somalia, Rwanda, and Haiti, as well as serving as a White House military aide responsible for carrying the President's Emergency Satchel, otherwise known as the "Nuclear Football," my family and I settled in my wife's native state of California.

When my wife was growing up, California was a middle-class paradise blessed with abundant natural resources, plentiful jobs, and an affordable, high standard of living. The state's politics were competitive and diverse. It was a state that often sent both a Democratic and a Republican senator to Washington.

Both parties had liberal, moderate, and conservative factions. It was a state that alternated between Republican and Democratic governors, giving us both Ronald Reagan and Jerry Brown. In national elections it was usually a Republican state. From 1952 to 1988, the state went to a Democratic presidential candidate only once (in 1964, when the state supported Lyndon Baines Johnson). In the twentieth century, it supported Republicans in every presidential election except in 1916, when it went for Woodrow Wilson; the four elections of Franklin Delano Roosevelt; and in 1948, when it voted for Truman. It was, in short, a classically American place that was full of people who pursued the American dream and shared basic American values, even as they ranged politically from the liberalism of the San Francisco Bay area to the hardcore conservatism of Orange County, and even as they differed culturally from the beach communities of the southern coast to the farmers of the rural Central Valley, and from the loggers of the northern forests to the cowboys of the inland desert.

But today, California has changed nearly beyond all recognition. It has undergone an historic, nearly unprecedented demographic revolution driven by unrestricted immigration. In 1960, about 92 percent of the state's population was classified as non-Hispanic white. By 2010, that number had fallen to about 40 percent. That's an astonishing transformation, and it continues. And with it have come other changes that have turned California from a middle-class paradise into something more like a Third World state with pockets of enormous wealth surrounded by extreme poverty. In fact, California—taking into consideration the cost of living—now has the *worst* poverty rate of any state in the nation (only the District of Columbia has a higher rate of poverty). Nearly *half* of America's homeless population is in California. Its great cities of San Francisco and Los Angeles are filled with litter, human waste, and the discarded needles of drug addicts, and they are sanctuaries for criminal illegal aliens. The state—once the center of a middle-class tax revolt—now has cripplingly high taxes, artificially high energy costs (combined with rolling blackouts that leave millions of Californians without power), and infrastructure that is collapsing. Politically, California is now a one-party state. And that one party—the Democratic Party—is no longer the diverse party of liberals, moderates, and conservatives that it once was; instead, it is a party of liberals and extreme leftists who are driving the biggest state in the United States into complete dysfunction.

And don't kid yourself—California is not an outlier. It is the future of the United States unless we regain control of our borders. If we don't, what does our future look like? It will be a future where an elite few continue to prosper and where, in gross numbers, the state and the country can continue to look like an economic powerhouse. But the reality for most of us—the reality outside elite, gated enclaves—will be something more like the Third World, where nothing works: not the light switch, not the water faucet, not the health care system, not the schools, nothing.

Sonny Bono, the singer who became a Republican congressman for California, was once asked his opinion of illegal immigration. He was pithy. He said simply, "When something is illegal, it's illegal. Enforce the law." Our elected officials—and sometimes the courts—have not done that. Instead, they have subverted the law, offering sanctuary and benefits to lawbreakers—and lawbreaking begets lawbreaking. Hard-pressed taxpayers are forced to subsidize services for non-legal residents. Adding insult *and* injury, Californians have also been forced to endure higher rates of crime than would be the case if our border were controlled. Writing in 2004, when sanctuary city policies were already becoming entrenched in big cities across the country, Heather Mac Donald noted, "In Los Angeles, 95 percent of all outstanding warrants for homicide…target illegal aliens. Up to two-thirds of all fugitive felony warrants…are for illegal aliens." In short, unrestricted immigration has imported crime, poverty, and even disease into California, lowering the standard of living and transforming the state's formerly robust two-party political culture into a "progressive" monoculture of failure.

Can anything be done about it? Yes, of course: These problems were created by politicians and could be fixed by them (if we had the right ones in office). But it won't be easy. It begins by restoring a respect for the rule of law, enforcing our nation's borders, and working hard to assimilate immigrants as America traditionally did with a catechism of patriotism and respect for the principles and values of the Constitution.

It is my earnest hope that this book, *Crisis on the Border*, will be read by members of Congress, by state legislators across the country, and by concerned citizens who recognize that enforcing our borders is, at bottom, an issue of national security. American citizenship is a precious gift, our country is a great one, and we will be held responsible by our children—and by history—if we let our sovereignty, our rule of law, and our constitutional republic slip away through the sheer negligence of not securing our borders. It doesn't have to be this way. All it takes is political will. And the political power to make change happen lies with us, as voters and as we the people, electing—and holding accountable—politicians who will actually strive to get the job done.

—Retired U.S. Air Force Lieutenant Colonel Robert "Buzz" Patterson, former senior military aide to the President of the United States

ACKNOWLEDGMENTS

I'd like to thank all the hardworking men and women I had the honor to serve with in Laredo. Their contributions to our nation's security and the rule of law never get enough credit. I'd also like to thank Austin Wright for his help with this book, as well as my wife, who provided the greatest help of all.

ALIEN INCARCERATION REPORT: JUNE 6, 2018

Alien Incarceration Report Fiscal Year 2018, Quarter 1

June 6, 2018

Alien Incarceration Report
Fiscal Year 2018, Quarter 1
June 6, 2018

On January 25, 2017, the President signed Executive Order (E.O.) 13768 on *Enhancing Public Safety in the Interior of the United States.*

Section 16 of the E.O. directs the U.S. Department of Homeland Security (DHS) and the U.S. Department of Justice (DOJ) to collect relevant data and provide quarterly reports on: (a) the immigration status of all aliens incarcerated under the supervision of the Federal Bureau of Prisons (BOP); (b) the immigration status of all aliens incarcerated as federal pretrial detainees under the supervision of the United States Marshals Service (USMS); and (c) the immigration status of all convicted aliens incarcerated in state prisons and local detention centers throughout the United States.

This report includes data on known or suspected aliens under the custody of BOP or USMS, and limited data regarding immigration status of convicted aliens incarcerated in state prisons and local detention centers throughout the United States. Future reports will also provide information regarding immigration status of aliens incarcerated in state prisons and local detention centers.

Summary of Findings

A total of 57,820 known or suspected aliens were in DOJ custody for a range of offenses at the end of the first quarter of Fiscal Year 2018 (FY18) (*see* Figure 1). Of those, 34,834 were confirmed aliens with orders of removal, 15,536 were still under investigation by ICE to determine alienage, 4,410 were aliens who were illegally present and undergoing removal proceedings, and 2,871 were legally present and undergoing removal proceedings. A total of 169 aliens in DOJ custody had been granted relief or protection from removal.

Figure 1: Immigration Status of Known or Suspected Aliens in DOJ Custody, FY2018 Q1

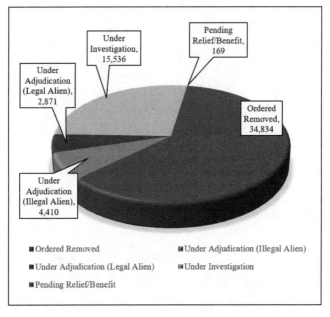

Source: U.S. Department of Justice, U.S. Department of Homeland Security

In an effort to facilitate as robust and thorough analysis as possible, this report expands the types and amounts of data provided pursuant to E.O. 13768. For example, it includes information regarding the costs to the criminal justice system relating to the incarceration of aliens (such as that it cost the USMS more than $134 million to house known or suspected aliens during the first quarter of FY18). DOJ and DHS will continue to improve their methodologies and policies for this report to improve the information they provide.

The prior quarterly report did not include data on the populations in state prisons or local jails, because comprehensive data regarding those individuals has not been routinely provided to DOJ or DHS by state or local authorities. This report includes some limited data on this topic, including aggregate data collected by DOJ, data reported directly to the public by state authorities, and other information made available through public reporting.

Nonetheless, the lack of comprehensive, comparable data in this area is a noteworthy limitation of this report, because state and local facilities account for approximately 90 percent of the total U.S. incarcerated population. DOJ and DHS are continuing to develop and establish methodologies and procedures that will allow them to collect, estimate, and analyze accurate data regarding the impact of aliens on public safety and criminal justice at the state and local levels. This section will continue to expand in future reports as these methodologies and procedures are finalized.

Process

Pursuant to E.O. 13768, USMS and BOP have begun providing U.S. Immigration and Customs Enforcement (ICE) with data on a quarterly basis regarding inmates and detainees identified as foreign-born during their criminal case process.[1] In turn, ICE checks USMS and BOP data against its ICE Enforcement and Removal Operations (ERO) case management system, the ENFORCE Alien Removal Module (EARM), and the U.S. Citizenship and Immigration Services Central Index System to identify aliens with immigration records and pending or completed removal proceedings.

This approach allows ICE to place each known or suspected alien within one of the following five categories:

- Under Investigation: Further investigation by ICE is required to confirm alien status and establish potential removability.
- Under Adjudication – Legal: The person is lawfully present in the United States but has been charged as a removable alien; removal proceedings are ongoing.
- Under Adjudication – Illegal: The person is unlawfully present[2] in the United States and has been charged as a removable alien; removal proceedings are ongoing.
- Ordered Removed: The person is an alien who has been issued a final order of removal and therefore has no lawful status.
- Relief/Benefit: The person is an alien who has been granted relief or protection from removal that would generally be considered lawful status. However, depending on the nature of the inmate's criminal offense, his or her status may be subject to review and rescission or revocation by DHS or an immigration judge.

Once ICE checks the USMS and BOP data, it returns its findings to USMS and BOP. That data is then utilized by USMS and BOP to generate statistics relevant to E.O. 13768, including the primary offenses committed, costs of incarceration, and other factors affecting public safety and criminal justice. USMS and BOP are continuing to develop their process to allow for more robust reporting of information related to E.O. 13768.

---

[1] Total counts in BOP and USMS custody reflect the populations on reported dates and are not quarterly or yearly totals.

[2] "Unlawful presence" includes those circumstances where an "alien is present in the United States after the expiration of the period of stay authorized … or is present in the United States without being admitted or paroled." 8 U.S.C. § 1182 (a)(9)(B)(ii).

Immigration Status of and Offenses Committed by Known or Suspected
Aliens in BOP Custody

A. Immigration Status of Known or Suspected Aliens in BOP Custody

As of December 30, 2017, a total of 38,132 known or suspected aliens were in BOP custody
(approximately 21 percent of the 183,058 total individuals in BOP custody on that date). More
than half (62 percent) did not have lawful immigration status in the United States. Of those,
20,976 (55 percent of the total number of known or suspected aliens in BOP custody) had been
ordered removed, and 2,850 (seven percent) were unlawfully present and in removal
proceedings. Approximately seven percent of the known or suspected aliens in BOP custody
(2,484 individuals) were lawfully present and in removal proceedings, and 124 aliens (less than
one percent) had received an immigration benefit or relief or protection from removal (*see* Figure
2).

ICE and BOP expect the proportion of aliens remaining in the "under investigation" status to
decline over time—a trend that was observed again in this quarter. As of December 2017, only
31 percent (11,698) of known or suspected aliens were under investigation, down from 38
percent in the fourth quarter and 50 percent in the third quarter.

Figure 2: Known or Suspected Aliens in BOP Custody, FY 2018 Q1

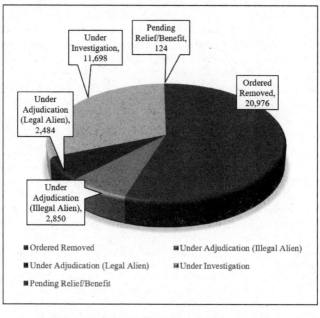

Source: U.S. Department of Justice, U.S. Department of Homeland Security

B. Primary Offenses Committed by Known or Suspected Aliens in BOP Custody

Approximately 46 percent (17,621) of known or suspected aliens in BOP custody had committed drug trafficking or other drug-related offenses (such as conspiracy to commit drug trafficking offenses, or smuggling large amounts of drugs on the high seas) as their primary offense, making it the most common type of offense. Of the 17,621 known or suspected aliens in BOP custody with a drug offense as their primary offense, only 107 (approximately one half of one percent) had a primary offense of simple possession—and many of these were traffickers who were caught with significant amounts of drugs but were convicted of lesser offenses as a result of circumstances such as plea bargains. The remaining 17,514 known or suspected aliens with a primary offense related to drugs (more than 99 percent of the total) were convicted of drug trafficking-related crimes.[3]

---

[3] The proportion of drug offenders sentenced for drug trafficking is generally consistent throughout the entire federal prison population. According to the Bureau of Justice Statistics, "[m]ore than 99% of federal drug offenders are sentenced for trafficking." *See* Bureau of Justice Statistics, *Prisoners in 2016* (Jan. 2018), https://www.bjs.gov/content/pub/pdf/p16.pdf.

Approximately 29 percent (10,912) of known or suspected aliens in BOP custody had committed immigration offenses (such as illegal reentry after deportation or human trafficking) as their primary offense. The third-largest category (approximately eight percent, or 3,161 individuals) of known or suspected aliens in BOP custody were those categorized as "Other," which is composed primarily of individuals awaiting trial. Drug trafficking-related and immigration offenses were the most common primary offenses associated with those in the "Other" category.

Of the known or suspected aliens in BOP custody, approximately four percent (1,673) had committed fraud as their primary offense (*see* Figure 3). Another four percent (1,486) committed weapons offenses (including firearms offenses). Racketeering and continuing criminal enterprise offenses (including murder for hire) were the primary offenses committed by approximately 3 percent (1,174), and obscene materials offenses (such as production or distribution of child pornography) and other sex offenses were the primary offenses committed by approximately 2 percent (782). Other primary offenses committed by smaller numbers of known or suspected aliens in BOP custody included kidnapping, murder, larceny, terrorism, escape, bribery and extortion, rape, and other offenses—aside from terrorism-related offenses, many of these types of offenses are typically prosecuted at the state and local level.

Future reports will also include information regarding costs associated with incarcerating aliens in BOP custody.

Figure 3: Primary Offenses Committed by Known or Suspected Aliens in BOP Custody, FY 2018 Q1

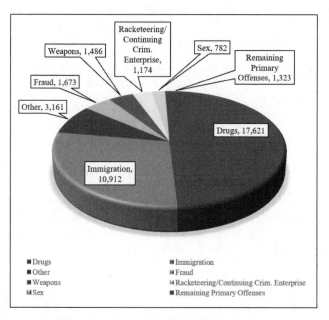

Source: U.S. Department of Justice, U.S. Department of Homeland Security

C. Examples of Newly Sentenced or Incarcerated Aliens in BOP Custody

The following are illustrative examples of aliens who were recently sentenced or incarcerated for federal offenses.

- **Adrian Pineda-Orozco** (W.D. Tex.), an illegal alien from Mexico, who was residing in Houston, Texas, was sentenced to 50 years in prison for his role in a scheme to smuggle over 43 kilograms of liquid methamphetamine into the United States. A jury convicted Pineda-Orozco of conspiracy to possess with intent to distribute methamphetamine and conspiracy to import methamphetamine. Pineda-Orozco's co-defendants pled guilty to conspiracy to possess with intent to distribute methamphetamine prior to trial.

  Evidence at trial established that Pineda-Orozco orchestrated a statewide methamphetamine importation and distribution scheme, with prior deliveries to Houston and Dallas. On December 15, 2015, Customs and Border Patrol (CBP) officers at the Eagle Pass Port of Entry discovered 15 plastic bottles containing liquid methamphetamine inside a vehicle being driven by the two co-defendants. One of the co-defendants confessed and told agents he was to deliver the methamphetamine to an individual in Houston. Agents then conducted a controlled delivery and discovered

Pineda-Orozco waiting for them in Houston. When agents identified themselves, Pineda-Orozco got into his vehicle and fled the scene, narrowly missing one of the agents. Pineda-Orozco led authorities on a high-speed chase through residential neighborhoods. The pursuit continued until spike strips disabled the vehicle. Pineda-Orozco was then arrested.

- **Anibel Rondolpho Rodriguez** (E.D.N.Y.), an illegal alien from Honduras, who was residing in Freeport, New York, was sentenced to 45 years in prison after he pled guilty to racketeering charges including two murder conspiracies, two attempted murders, and threatening to commit assault.

    o On August 9, 2012, Rodriguez, a member of Mara Salvatrucha (MS-13), agreed with two co-conspirators to kill M. P., who was associated with the Zulu Nation gang. The Zulu Nation had an ongoing dispute with members of the Hempstead Locos Salvatruchas, a clique of MS-13. While the defendant was talking to the victim, a co-conspirator fatally shot the victim three times with a 9 mm handgun.
    o On October 6, 2013, the defendant and six co-defendants confronted J. I. R.-L. about his suspected membership in a rival gang. The defendant and his co-conspirators decided to kill R.-L. and R.-L.'s friend, who was a potential witness. R.-L. was fatally stabbed more than two dozen times, and his friend was stabbed 18 times but survived.
    o On September 14, 2013, the defendant with other MS-13 gang members confronted John Doe and another individual whom they believed were members of a rival Bloods street gang. The defendant grabbed a baseball bat and struck John Doe. Others also struck John Doe with a wooden board, stabbed him with a screwdriver, and punched and kicked him. John Doe survived.
    o On October 6, 2013, the defendant and other MS-13 gang members approached John Doe 2 and asked him whether he was a gang member, questioning him about a tattoo on his arm. When John Doe 2 denied gang membership and tried to walk away, he was stabbed and kicked by the defendant and his MS-13 gang friends.

- **Eduardo Martinez** (N.D. Ind.), an illegal alien residing in Fort Wayne, Indiana, was sentenced to 324 months in prison after he pled guilty to possession with intent to distribute more than a kilogram of heroin, distribution of more than 50 grams of methamphetamine, and possession of a firearm by an illegal alien. According to court documents, Martinez distributed methamphetamine, cocaine, and marijuana from July 2013 through December 2014. From calls intercepted pursuant to a federally authorized warrant, agents learned that in November and December 2014, Martinez coordinated an incoming shipment of multiple kilograms of heroin. The investigation concluded with the seizure of that shipment, wherein Martinez received a portion of the shipment. Martinez and six other co-defendants were arrested.

- **Paula Villalva-Patricio** (S.D. Miss.), a citizen of Mexico, was sentenced to 180 months in prison after a jury found her guilty of conspiracy to commit an offense against the United States, attempting to smuggle firearms out of the United States in violation of regulations and laws, and transporting or delivering firearms to a person who does not reside in the same state. In August 2011, a Jackson County Sheriff's deputy stopped a truck. During a search of that truck, the deputy found two firearms and flak jackets hidden in a spare tire. In November 2011, in a subsequent traffic stop of the same truck, deputies uncovered an additional 28 firearms and 600 rounds of ammunition secreted under the truck bed. Further investigation led to the identification of Villalva-Patricio in September 2012. She was later apprehended in November 2016, while crossing into the United States at the border in San Diego, California.

- **Celin Javier Montoya-Rodriguez** (S.D. Tex.), a lawful permanent resident from Mexico, and **Jonathon Sanchez-Torres**, an illegal alien from Mexico who was residing in Pharr, Texas, were sentenced to 120 months each after pleading guilty to two counts of unlawfully transferring destructive devices. Bureau of Alcohol, Tobacco, Firearms and Explosives (ATF) and ICE Homeland Security Investigations (HSI) agents conducted a lengthy investigation that included undercover operations that exposed a conspiracy to manufacture military-style grenades, which were to be sold and exported to Mexico. Over a six-month period, one of four other co-defendants, Gonzalez, acquired all of the components necessary to construct more than 150 improvised hand grenades, including grenade hulls, spring kits, fuses, and black powder, from a combination of online merchants and local stores. Gonzalez assembled the grenades in a workshop located behind his home.

As the grenades were completed, Sanchez-Torres delivered batches of the live hand grenades to co-defendant Vega-Genova. Vega-Genova worked with Montoya-Rodriguez, Ozuna and Rivera to sell the grenades. Between November 5, 2016, and November 9, 2016, on four separate occasions, agents purchased 45 grenades directly from Vega, Montoya-Rodriguez, Ozuna and Rivera at a cost of $400-$450 per grenade. Subsequent surveillance and undercover operations led to the discovery of the identity and location of the grenade manufacturer – Gonzalez. Agents learned that prior to the start of the investigation, the defendants had manufactured and sold approximately 50 grenades to other unknown individuals who were exporting the grenades to Mexico. At the time of his arrest, Gonzalez was in the process of acquiring components to manufacture an additional 200 grenades. Agents were able to intercept some of the component parts that were being shipped to Gonzalez's residence.

- **Santos Portillo Andrade** (D. Mass), aka "Flaco," a lawful permanent resident from El Salvador residing in Revere, Massachusetts, was sentenced to 10 years in prison after he pled guilty to a RICO conspiracy involving an aggravated assault, conspiracy to possess with intent to distribute heroin and cocaine, and possession of a firearm in furtherance of drug trafficking. Andrade, the leader of MS-13's East Boston Loco Salvatrucha clique, admitted that he was engaged in a conspiracy to conduct enterprise affairs through a pattern of racketeering activity, which included admitting responsibility for an aggravated assault on an individual he believed was a rival gang member in Malden, Massachusetts, in December 2008. Andrade also admitted that he conspired to distribute at least 100 grams of heroin and 500 grams of cocaine. In addition, Andrade admitted that he possessed a firearm in furtherance of his drug trafficking.

- **Pedro Quintero-Enriques** (S.D. Ala.), aka, Miguel Angel Quintero, an illegal alien from Mexico who was residing in Summerdale, Alabama, was sentenced to 108 months in prison after he pled guilty to illegal reentry after deportation and felon in possession of firearms. Quintero-Enriques is a convicted felon who illegally reentered the United States on numerous occasions. In 2002, he was convicted in the United States District Court for the Southern District of Texas for illegal entry. On January 23, 2012, he was deported. He then reentered the country, and in October 2013, he was indicted for illegal reentry in the Southern District of Alabama. He was sentenced to time served and again deported. Notwithstanding his previous deportations, Quintero-Enriques unlawfully returned to the United States several times. He was deported again in August 2013, and November 2014. His criminal history includes domestic violence. As a convicted felon and illegal alien, he is prohibited from possessing firearms.

  o On October 16, 2016, Baldwin County Sheriff's deputies responded to a domestic violence call at the home of Quintero-Enriques. Upon their arrival, deputies saw two firearms, in plain view, in a blue Ford F-150 truck, which was parked underneath the home's awning. Deputies met and spoke with Quintero-Enriques who allowed deputies to enter his home. Agents saw drug residue and drug paraphernalia upon entry into the house. Deputies later arrested Quintero-Enriques. Deputies also seized two firearms, from the truck, which included a pump shotgun and a Ruger mini-14 rifle. The shotgun was loaded and contained four shells. After a search of Quintero-Enriques, deputies found in his wallet two North Carolina I.D. cards that appeared to be fake and approximately $1,785 cash. Quintero-Enriques admitted that he was in the country illegally.

- **Martel Valencia-Cortez** (S.D. Cal.), an illegal alien from Mexico and prolific alien smuggler, was sentenced to 99 months in prison for hurling a softball-sized rock at a U.S. Border Patrol agent and for alien smuggling. A jury convicted Valencia-Cortez of assault on a federal officer with a deadly weapon and three counts of bringing in an illegal alien for financial gain. The defendant had been on supervised release for a 2013 alien smuggling conviction at the time he committed the new offenses.

  On November 15, 2015, less than two months after his last deportation to Mexico following the completion of a 33-month sentence for his prior alien smuggling conviction, Valencia re-entered the United States guiding a group of 15 undocumented aliens. When agents discovered the group, Valencia threw a softball-sized rock from a distance of approximately 30 feet that hit an agent on the side of the agent's face. Valencia then fled to back into Mexico. Agents arrested Valencia when Mexican authorities escorted him to the San Ysidro Port of Entry on March 11, 2016. At trial, the Border Patrol victim testified that he had never been hit that hard in his life and that he felt an overwhelming pain that caused him to feel dazed and disoriented, as if he was going to pass out. The rock hit the agent so hard that he thought his teeth had been knocked out or his jaw had been broken.

- **Miguel Cabrera-Rangel** (S.D. Tex.), an illegal alien from Mexico, was sentenced to 96 months in prison after a jury convicted him of assault on a federal officer. Evidence at trial demonstrated that a Border Patrol agent responded to a report of a possible group of illegal aliens on a ranch near Hebbronville. The agent came upon the group and attempted to apprehend them. Cabrera was one of the illegal aliens. To avoid apprehension, Cabrera engaged the agent in a physical struggle during which Cabrera grabbed the agent's flashlight. Cabrera punched the agent in the face and then struck the agent with the flashlight causing a bilateral fracture of the nose along with lacerations and contusions. Cabrera then fled but was later apprehended on a fishing boat in Copano Bay, near Corpus Christi. At sentencing, the victim informed the court that he had continuing issues with his eye. He suffered a detached retina and also developed cataracts.

Immigration Status of and Pending Charges Against Known or Suspected Aliens in USMS Custody

A. Immigration Status of Known or Suspected Aliens in USMS Custody

The USMS is DOJ's component charged with the housing and care of federal pretrial detainees. USMS also houses certain short-term sentenced individuals, as well as sentenced individuals pending transfer to BOP. This report includes data on all known or suspected aliens in USMS custody.[4] As of December 31, 2017, 19,688 confirmed aliens were in USMS custody, along with 3,022 individuals for whom alienage had not yet been determined.

Confirmed aliens, identified through self-reporting or through confirmation of alienage by ICE, comprised 37 percent of the 53,141 total individuals in USMS custody. Of those aliens, 70 percent (13,858 individuals) had removal orders, 19 percent (3,838 individuals) had their immigration status currently under investigation, and nearly eight percent (1,560 individuals) were unlawfully present and in removal proceedings (*see* Figure 4). Only two percent (387 individuals) of the confirmed aliens in USMS custody were lawfully present and in immigration proceedings. Only 45 aliens in USMS custody were in receipt of a grant of protection or relief from removal.

---

[4] USMS data reflects all aliens in USMS custody, and does not delineate solely pretrial aliens as the USMS also detains post-trial aliens completing short-term sentences or awaiting transfer to BOP.

Figure 4: Immigration Status of Confirmed Aliens in USMS Custody, FY2018 Q1

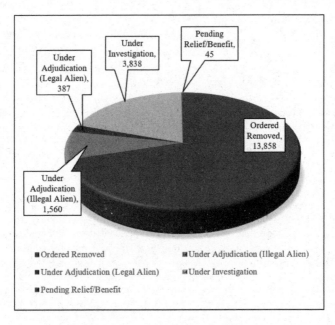

Source: U.S. Department of Justice, U.S. Department of Homeland Security

B. Pending Primary Charges Against Confirmed Aliens in USMS Custody

Of the 19,688 aliens in USMS custody, approximately 56 percent (10,971 individuals) were in custody for a primary offense related to immigration, such as human trafficking or illegal reentry after deportation (*see* Figure 5). Approximately 24 percent (4,665 individuals) of aliens in USMS custody were in custody for a primary offense related to drugs. Other primary offenses included violations of conditions of supervision (974 individuals, approximately five percent of aliens in USMS custody), property offenses (889 individuals, approximately five percent of aliens in USMS custody), weapons offenses, and violent offenses (391 and 378 individuals, respectively, each approximately two percent of aliens in USMS custody). Approximately four percent (745 individuals) of aliens in USMS custody were material witnesses.

Notably, 68 percent (13,449) of all aliens in USMS custody were apprehended in the southwest region.

Figure 5: Pending Primary Charges Against Confirmed Aliens in USMS Custody, FY2018 Q1

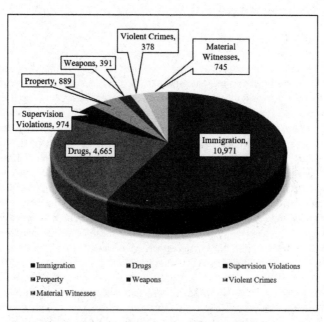

Source: U.S. Department of Justice, U.S. Department of Homeland Security

C. Costs Associated With Confirmed Aliens in USMS Custody

During the first quarter of FY18, USMS had an average daily population of 19,472 confirmed aliens in custody, and incurred more than $134 million in housing costs related to those prisoners during that quarter. An average of 3,175 of those aliens were held in BOP facilities, and for whom no direct housing costs were incurred by USMS (the costs were instead funded by appropriations received by BOP). An average daily population of 65 aliens were also housed in settings for which no direct housing costs were incurred by USMS, such as in hospitals or in correctional health care facilities due to required medical treatment. The remaining 16,233 aliens (daily average) in USMS custody were housed in a combination of state, local, and private facilities, at an average cost of $89.84 per diem.

Immigration Status of Individuals in State and Local Custody

Through its Office of Justice Programs ("OJP"), Bureau of Justice Statistics ("BJS"), DOJ continues its progress towards establishing a data collection of the immigration status of convicted aliens incarcerated in state prisons and local detention centers. In the meantime, some data is already available from particular states, such as Texas. Additionally, some information is available through public reporting of cases that offer anecdotal evidence of alien criminal activity at the state and local levels.

A. Gathering Data from State Prisons

BJS currently collects on an annual basis aggregate numbers of noncitizens in state and federal prisons through the National Prisoner Statistics ("NPS") program. The respective departments of corrections voluntarily submit these numbers. The most recent records, released in January 2018, were from December 31, 2016. According to that report, there were approximately 83,573 inmates under federal jurisdiction or in state custody who are not U.S. citizens. As BJS appropriately noted,[5] state numbers in the report, which reflect 43,617 noncitizen individuals in custody, represent an undercount, because five states—including California, Nevada, and Oregon—did not report citizenship data. In addition, other states likely also provided undercounts, in part because; (1) inmates self-report place of birth or citizenship, and state corrections departments use these elements differently to determine citizenship, and (2) the count for most states only includes individuals in state-run institutions, not private facilities. Due to this underreporting (or complete lack of reporting) by some states, the aggregate tally of 83,573 noncitizen inmates reported to BJS as being under federal jurisdiction or in state custody does not currently represent a comprehensive national total.

BJS is improving its data collection in this area, including asking states and the BOP to provide additional information to disaggregate the number of noncitizens in custody by basic sentence length and by sex as of December 31 each year. The enhanced data collection began in January 2018, and will also include counts of noncitizens in both state-run and private facilities for all jurisdictions. BJS expects to release the 2017 counts of noncitizens in the fall of 2018. BJS is also continuing its efforts to modify the National Corrections Reporting Program ("NCRP"), BJS's annual collection of individual-level state prisoner records, to collect citizenship status of all inmates in state prisons.

B. Gathering Data from Local Detention Facilities

BJS currently collects data from local detention facilities through its Annual Survey of Jails ("ASJ"). Currently, the ASJ data cannot be used to accurately estimate the total number of noncitizens in local custody. BJS is working to improve reporting from local facilities, and develop ASJ's data collection to allow the disaggregation of conviction status, which would enable analysis of ASJ data to determine the number of noncitizens in custody, and to break those numbers down by conviction status. During the first quarter of FY18, BJS fielded a pilot study to investigate the ability of local jail facilities to report this information.

In addition, the Department of Homeland Security, Office of Immigration Statistics is currently evaluating potential strategies to estimate the immigration status of individuals in state and local

---

[5] Bureau of Justice Statistics, *Prisoners in 2016* (Jan. 2018), https://www.bjs.gov/content/pub/pdf/p16.pdf.

custody based on information available in the U.S. Census Bureau's American Community Survey on individuals living in institutional settings, a category that includes federal and state prisons as well as local jails.

C. Nonfederal Data and Public Reporting

While the Departments of Justice and Homeland Security are developing improved methods to collect and analyze relevant data from state and local authorities, some already take the proactive step of making this data available to the public.

For example, the Texas Department of Public Safety publishes data online regarding criminal alien arrests and convictions. These data do not account for all aliens in the Texas criminal justice system, as they are limited to criminal alien arrestees who have had prior interaction with DHS resulting in the collection of their fingerprints. Nonetheless, these data are helpful in understanding how criminal aliens impact public safety and criminal justice. As reported by Texas Department of Public Safety:

> According to DHS status indicators, over 251,000 criminal aliens have been booked into local Texas jails between June 1, 2011 and April 30, 2018. During their criminal careers, these criminal aliens were charged with more than 663,000 criminal offenses. Those arrests include 1,351 homicide charges; 79,049 assault charges; 18,685 burglary charges; 79,900 drug charges; 815 kidnapping charges; 44,882 theft charges; 50,777 obstructing police charges; 4,292 robbery charges; 7,156 sexual assault charges; and 9,938 weapon charges. Of the total criminal aliens arrested in that timeframe, over 168,000 or 66% were identified by DHS status as being in the US illegally at the time of their last arrest.

> According to DPS criminal history records, those criminal charges have thus far resulted in over 296,000 convictions including 583 homicide convictions; 29,768 assault convictions; 9,202 burglary convictions; 39,002 drug convictions; 282 kidnapping convictions; 20,355 theft convictions; 24,836 obstructing police convictions; 2,245 robbery convictions; 3,317 sexual assault convictions; and 4,117 weapon convictions. Of the convictions associated with criminal alien arrests, over 197,000 or 66% are associated with aliens who were identified by DHS status as being in the US illegally at the time of their last arrest.[6]

D. Examples of Crimes Committed by Aliens at the State and Local Level

In addition to official data from state and local authorities, media reports can be helpful in understanding the impacts of aliens on public safety and criminal justice in the United States.

---

[6] *Texas Criminal Alien Arrest Data*, Texas Dep't of Pub. Safety (last visited May 24, 2018), https://www.dps.texas.gov/administration/crime_records/pages/txCriminalAlienStatistics.htm.

Media reports are inherently less desirable than official data, in part because of the higher possibility of inaccuracies. Additionally, media reports are limited in their utility to identify larger trends, both because the reporting may be inconsistent and because media reports may be more likely to report on atypically serious crimes. Nonetheless, particularly in absence of official data, anecdotal examples from public reporting can help develop the issue. A few examples from the first quarter of FY18 include:[7]

- **Miguel "Timido" Angel Lopez-Abrego**, 19, who was charged with first-degree murder for his alleged involvement in an MS-13 attack in Wheaton, Maryland., in which as many as 10 MS-13 members lured a man into a park, stabbed him more than 100 times, decapitated him, and then cut out his heart. Lopez-Abrego is a native of El Salvador in the United States illegally.[8]

- **Kula Pelima**, 30, who confessed to police that she drowned two children, four-months old and five years old, respectively, in a bathtub. Pelima is a Liberian native who had lived in the United States for two decades.[9]

- **Leonel Vazquez**, 34, who pleaded guilty to sexually abusing an underage, developmentally delayed girl in Kentucky. Vazquez was first arrested for the charge in June 2017, but in November 2017 it was revealed that he was an illegal alien who had been deported at least twice before.[10]

- **Hugo Parral-Aguirre**, 30, who was arrested after allegedly shooting a county sheriff's deputy in the shoulder with a shotgun in California, and allegedly attempting to shoot another individual earlier that same day. Parral-Aguirre is a Mexican national in the United States illegally, and had been previously deported.[11]

---

[7] The information contained within these examples comes entirely from the cited media reports. Neither DOJ nor DHS make any assurances as to the accuracy of the information provided in these examples, nor have DOJ or DHS independently confirmed any of the information in this section. The examples are provided solely for the purpose of demonstrating the type of information that is often contained within media reports about criminal activity.

[8] Dan Morse, *Police: MS-13 members in Maryland stab man more than 100 times and decapitate him*, Washington Post (Nov. 22, 2017), https://www.washingtonpost.com/local/public-safety/police-ms-13-members-in-maryland-stab-man-more-than-100-times-and-decapitate-him/2017/11/22/0cba9760-cf7e-11e7-a1a3-0d1e45a6de3d_story.html.

[9] *Mom, fearing deportation, drowns infant son, 5-year-old half-brother, cops say*, FOXNEWS.com (Oct. 18, 2017), http://www.foxnews.com/us/2017/10/18/mom-fearing-deportation-drowns-infant-son-5-year-old-half-brother-cops-say.html.

[10] Amanda Roberts, *Illegal immigrant facing deportation for 3rd time after sexual assault*, WPSD (NBC local affiliate) (Nov. 14, 2017), http://www.wpsdlocal6.com/2017/11/14/illegal-immigrant-facing-deportation-3rd-time-sexual-assault/.

[11] Will Houston, *Sheriff: Suspect in shooting of Humboldt County deputy previously deported*, Eureka Times-Standard (Dec. 18, 2017), http://www.times-standard.com/general-news/20171218/sheriff-suspect-in-shooting-of-humboldt-county-deputy-previously-deported.

- **Estuardo Rufino Chaves**, 23, who was sentenced to five years in prison in New Jersey for second-degree reckless death by automobile as part of a plea bargain after he killed a motorcyclist. ICE placed a detainer on Chaves, a Guatemalan national, after his arrest.[12]

- **Hugo Giron-Polanco**, 38, who was arrested in December 2017 in connection with an alleged 2010 rape case in Florida when his DNA was matched with a sample collected from the victim. Giron-Polanco is a native of El Salvador in the United States illegally.[13]

Additional Information Regarding Criminal Aliens in the United States

A. Efforts to Expand the Institutional Hearing and Removal Program

The Institutional Hearing and Removal Program (IHRP) is a cooperative effort between the Executive Office for Immigration Review (EOIR), DHS, and various federal, state, and municipal corrections agencies. As part of the IHRP, DHS identifies alien inmates in BOP, state, or local custody who may be removable from the United States and initiates their removal proceedings before EOIR while the aliens continue serving their criminal sentences. Bringing immigration judges to these inmates for a determination of their removability allows their immigration case to be resolved prior to their release from incarceration. Through the IHRP, EOIR provides in-person and video teleconference immigration proceedings to determine whether alien inmates are removable from the United States and, if removable, whether they are eligible for any form of protection or relief from removal.

Upon their release from custody, DHS is able to effectuate the removal of those aliens who have a final order of removal, as determined by either an immigration judge or the Board of Immigration Appeals. IHRP aims to avoid transferring removable aliens into DHS custody, or releasing them into the community, pending future adjudication of their immigration case. By holding immigration proceedings during an alien's prison sentence, IHRP enhances the overall efficiency of the immigration system while contributing to the Nation's security.

Between October 1 and December 31, 2017, EOIR completed 851 immigration cases at 47 IHRP locations. EOIR had 1660 IHRP cases pending as of December 31, 2017 and may hear cases at additional IHRP locations as circumstances warrant.

---

[12] Sulaiman Abdur-Rahman, *Illegal immigrant gets 5 years for Hopewell Township vehicular homicide*, The Trentonian (Oct. 27, 2017), http://www.trentonian.com/general-news/20171027/illegal-immigrant-gets-5-years-for-hopewell-township-vehicular-homicide.

[13] Tonya Alanez, *Davie police say they have solved 2010 rape case*, Sun Sentinel (Dec. 29, 2017), http://www.sun-sentinel.com/local/broward/davie/fl-sb-rape-cold-case-arrest-20171228-story.html.

ALIEN INCARCERATION REPORT: APRIL 16, 2019

Alien Incarceration Report
Fiscal Year 2018, Quarter 2

April 16, 2019

Alien Incarceration Report
Fiscal Year 2018, Quarter 2

April 16, 2019

On January 25, 2017, the President signed Executive Order (E.O.) 13768 on *Enhancing Public Safety in the Interior of the United States.*

Section 16 of the E.O. directs the U.S. Department of Homeland Security (DHS) and the U.S. Department of Justice (DOJ) to collect relevant data and provide quarterly reports on: (a) the immigration status of all aliens incarcerated under the supervision of the Federal Bureau of Prisons (BOP); (b) the immigration status of all aliens incarcerated as federal pretrial detainees under the supervision of the United States Marshals Service (USMS); and (c) the immigration status of all convicted aliens incarcerated in state prisons and local detention centers throughout the United States.

This report includes data on known or suspected aliens under the custody of BOP or USMS, and limited data regarding the immigration status of convicted aliens incarcerated in state prisons and local detention centers throughout the United States. Future reports will also provide additional information regarding the immigration status of aliens incarcerated in state prisons and local detention centers.

Summary of Findings

A total of 59,945 known or suspected aliens were in DOJ custody for a range of offenses at the end of the second quarter of Fiscal Year 2018 (FY18) (*see* Figure 1). Of those, 36,235 were confirmed aliens with orders of removal or who had agreed to depart voluntarily, 16,426 were still under investigation by ICE to determine alienage, 4,903 were aliens who were illegally present and undergoing removal proceedings, and 1,281 were legally present and undergoing removal proceedings. A total of 1,100 aliens in DOJ custody had been granted relief or protection from removal.

Figure 1: Immigration Status of Known or Suspected Aliens in DOJ Custody, FY18 Q2

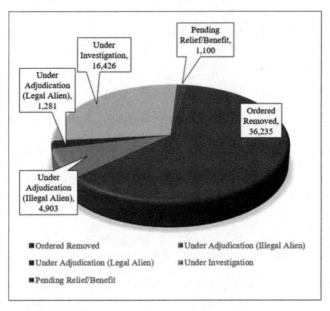

Source: U.S. Department of Justice, U.S. Department of Homeland Security

This report also includes the available data regarding alien populations in state and local facilities, including aggregate data collected by DOJ, data reported directly to the public by state authorities, and other information made available through public reporting. The lack of comprehensive data on this topic is a noteworthy limitation of this report, because state and local facilities account for approximately 90 percent of the total U.S. incarcerated population. DOJ and DHS are continuing to develop and establish methods to collect, estimate, and analyze accurate data regarding the impact of aliens on public safety and the criminal justice system at the state and local levels. This section of the report will continue to expand as these methodologies and procedures are improved or more information becomes available.

Process

Pursuant to E.O. 13768, USMS and BOP provide U.S. Immigration and Customs Enforcement (ICE) with data on a quarterly basis regarding inmates and detainees identified as foreign-born during their criminal case process.[1] In turn, ICE checks USMS and BOP data against its ICE Enforcement and Removal Operations (ERO) case management system, the ENFORCE Alien

---

[1] Total counts in BOP and USMS custody reflect the populations on reported dates and are not quarterly or yearly totals.

Removal Module (EARM), and the U.S. Citizenship and Immigration Services Central Index System to identify aliens with immigration records and pending or completed removal proceedings.

This approach allows ICE to place each known or suspected alien within one of the following five categories:

- Under Investigation: Further investigation by ICE is required to confirm alien status and establish potential removability.
- Under Adjudication – Legal: The person is lawfully present in the United States but has been charged as a removable alien; removal proceedings are ongoing.
- Under Adjudication – Illegal: The person is unlawfully present[2] in the United States and has been charged as a removable alien; removal proceedings are ongoing.
- Ordered Removed: The person is an alien who has been issued a final order of removal or has agreed to depart voluntarily, and therefore has no lawful status.
- Relief/Benefit: The person is an alien who has been granted relief or protection from removal that would generally be considered lawful status. However, depending on the nature of the inmate's criminal offense, his or her status may be subject to review and rescission or revocation by DHS or an immigration judge.

Once ICE checks the USMS and BOP data, it returns its findings to USMS and BOP. That data is then utilized by USMS and BOP to generate statistics relevant to E.O. 13768, including the primary offenses committed, costs of incarceration, and other factors affecting public safety and the criminal justice system. USMS and BOP are continuing to develop their process to allow for more robust reporting of information related to E.O. 13768.

Immigration Status of and Offenses Committed by Known or Suspected Aliens in BOP Custody

A. Immigration Status of Known or Suspected Aliens in BOP Custody

As of March 31, 2018, 38,391 known or suspected aliens were in BOP custody (approximately 21 percent of the 183,291 total individuals in BOP custody on that date). More than half of the 38,391 known or suspected aliens (approximately 64 percent) were confirmed not to have lawful immigration status in the United States, including 21,170 (55 percent of the total number of known or suspected aliens in BOP custody) who had been ordered removed, and 3,316 (nearly nine percent) who were unlawfully present and in removal proceedings. Nearly three percent of the known or suspected aliens in BOP custody (1,007 individuals) were lawfully present and in

---

[2] "Unlawful presence" includes those circumstances where an "alien is present in the United States after the expiration of the period of stay authorized … or is present in the United States without being admitted or paroled." 8 U.S.C. § 1182(a)(9)(B)(ii).

removal proceedings, and 855 aliens (approximately two percent) had received an immigration benefit or relief or protection from removal (*see* Figure 2).

DOJ and DHS expect the proportion of aliens remaining in the "under investigation" status to continue to decline over time. As of March 2018, only 31 percent (12,043) of the known or suspected aliens were under investigation, approximately the same percentage as in the first quarter of FY18, and down from the third and fourth quarters of FY17 (50 percent and 38 percent, respectively).

Figure 2: Known or Suspected Aliens in BOP Custody, FY18 Q2

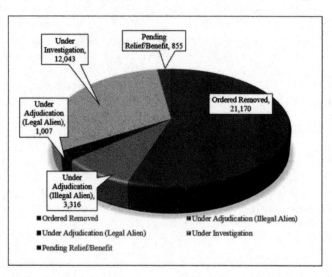

Source: U.S. Department of Justice, U.S. Department of Homeland Security

B. Primary Offenses Committed by Known or Suspected Aliens in BOP Custody

Approximately 46 percent (17,540) of the known or suspected aliens in BOP custody committed drug trafficking or other drug-related offenses (such as conspiracy to commit drug trafficking offenses, or smuggling large amounts of drugs on the high seas) as their primary offense, making it the most common type of offense (*see* Figure 3). Of the 17,540 known or suspected aliens in BOP custody with a drug offense as their primary offense, 17,354 (approximately 99 percent) were convicted of drug trafficking or other drug trafficking-related crimes. Only 186 (approximately one percent of the known or suspected aliens with a drug offense as their primary offense) had a primary offense of simple possession—and many of these were traffickers who were caught with significant amounts of drugs but were convicted of lesser offenses as a result of circumstances such as plea bargains.[3]

Approximately 28 percent (10,693) of the known or suspected aliens in BOP custody had committed immigration offenses (such as human trafficking or illegal reentry after deportation) as their primary offense. The third-largest category (approximately nine percent, or 3,582 individuals) of known or suspected aliens in BOP custody were individuals awaiting trial. Drug trafficking-related and immigration offenses were the most common primary charges associated with those in the pre-trial category.

Of the known or suspected aliens in BOP custody, approximately five percent (1,737) had committed fraud as their primary offense. Another four percent (1,480) committed weapons offenses (including firearms offenses). Racketeering and continuing criminal enterprise offenses (including murder for hire) were the primary offenses committed by approximately 3 percent (1,194), and obscene materials offenses (such as the production or distribution of child pornography) and other sex offenses were the primary offenses committed by approximately 2 percent (820). Other primary offenses committed by smaller numbers of known or suspected aliens in BOP custody included kidnapping, murder, larceny, terrorism, escape, bribery and extortion, rape, and other offenses—aside from terrorism-related offenses, many of these types of offenses are typically prosecuted at the state and local level.

Future reports will also include information regarding costs associated with incarcerating aliens in BOP custody.

---

[3] The proportion of drug offenders sentenced for drug trafficking is generally consistent throughout the entire federal prison population. According to the Bureau of Justice Statistics, "[m]ore than 99% of federal drug offenders are sentenced for trafficking." *See* Bureau of Justice Statistics, *Prisoners in 2016* (Jan. 2018), https://www.bjs.gov/content/pub/pdf/p16.pdf.

Figure 3: Primary Offenses Committed by Known or Suspected
Aliens in BOP Custody, FY18 Q2

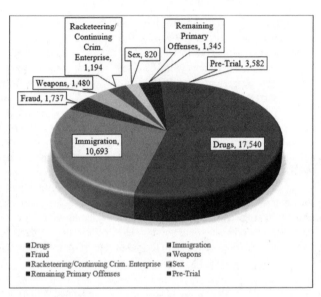

Source: U.S. Department of Justice, U.S. Department of Homeland Security

C. Examples of Newly Sentenced or Incarcerated Aliens in BOP Custody

The following are examples of aliens who were recently sentenced or incarcerated for federal offenses.

- **Yovanny Aroldo Mendivil-Balderama** (W.D. Mo.), 23, a Mexican national who resided in Missouri, was sentenced to 50 years in federal prison, after he pled guilty to participating in a conspiracy to distribute methamphetamine in Greene, Dallas, Webster and Christian counties in Missouri, from April 2015 through April 2016. He also pled guilty to using a firearm in furtherance of a drug-trafficking crime, resulting in the murder of Oscar Adan Martinez-Gaxiola on April 25, 2016.

According to court documents, Mendivil-Balderama and Martinez-Gaxiola obtained large amounts of methamphetamine from either Arizona or Mexico and transported it to Missouri. They supplied methamphetamine to co-defendant Brooke Danielle Beckley, 21, of Nixa, Missouri, for distribution in the Springfield area. On April 6, 2016, law enforcement officers seized from Beckley's hotel room approximately 1.9 kilograms of methamphetamine, a loaded 20-gauge shotgun with a sawed off barrel and stock, four rounds of additional shotgun ammunition, a .22-caliber pistol, a drug ledger, and $3,663. The seizure of the 1.9 kilograms of methamphetamine created a $44,000 debt that

Beckley owed to both Mendivil-Balderama and Martinez-Gaxiola. Text messages between Mendivil-Balderama and Beckley later established that they both wanted to kill Martinez-Gaxiola as a way to reduce, or extend, the debt, and to prevent Martinez-Gaxiola from possibly killing Beckley. Beckley recruited other co-defendants to carry out the murder.

On April 25, 2016, Mendivil-Balderama traveled with Martinez-Gaxiola to a co-defendant's residence on the pretext that Beckley would pay the drug debt. Beckley and the other co-defendants were waiting at the residence. Upon arrival, Mendivil-Balderama got out of the vehicle first. When Martinez-Gaxiola exited the vehicle, the other co-defendants opened fire, expending 30 to 60 rounds of ammunition, and Martinez-Gaxiola fell to the ground. One of the co-defendants then went up to where Martinez-Gaxiola lay and shot him once in the head. Martinez-Gaxiola was later found to have been armed with a handgun but did not discharge it during his murder. Neighbors reported the shots fired. As police responded to the area, the defendants attempted to conceal Martinez-Gaxiola's body by hiding him under a piece of tin siding. They all then fled. Officers found Martinez-Gaxiola alive but he died before they could transport him to the hospital.

- **Sergio Chavez-Verduzco** and his son, **Sergio Chavez-Macias** (D. Idaho), both Mexican nationals living in Burley, Idaho, were sentenced to 420 months and 144 months in prison after a jury convicted them of conspiracy related to drug trafficking. Chavez-Verduzco was also sentenced for his participation in a continuing criminal enterprise. Evidence presented during the trial showed that from 2015 and early 2016, Chavez-Verduzco and Chavez-Macias were the source of supply for multiple large-scale methamphetamine traffickers in the Treasure Valley of Idaho. The evidence specifically identified certain methamphetamine traffickers whom the father and son supplied with hundreds of pounds of methamphetamine.

- **Ramiro Hermosillo-Salazar** (N.D. Ga.), a Mexican national residing in Palmetto, Georgia, was sentenced to 30 years in prison after he pled guilty to conspiracy and possession of methamphetamine with intent to distribute, possession of methamphetamine with intent to distribute on premises where minor children resided, and possession of firearms in furtherance of drug trafficking crimes. As presented in court, following a multi-month DEA investigation, agents identified Hermosillo-Salazar as a likely member of a methamphetamine trafficking organization.

On June 15, 2017, DEA agents, aided by the Coweta County Sheriff's Office S.W.A.T. team, executed a federal search warrant at Hermosillo's residence in Palmetto. Law enforcement encountered the defendant in his residence and arrested him. They discovered that Hermosillo was also living with his three minor children, ages 5, 8, and 9. During the search, agents discovered a methamphetamine "superlab" in a separate building several yards from the house. The lab contained approximately 300 pounds of highly pure crystal methamphetamine, as well as several gallons of liquid methamphetamine that, if converted to its crystal form, would have yielded an additional 100 pounds of the drug. Inside the residence, agents found a second, smaller methamphetamine lab in a room next to the kitchen. They also found several more kilograms of methamphetamine and over $12,000. Hermosillo had placed three loaded rifles at points throughout the home, one of which was equipped with a high-capacity magazine. Hermosillo also had a bulletproof vest. A video-surveillance system revealed that Hermosillo had been operating the "superlab" for at least several months. Hermosillo was ordered to pay restitution to the government for the cost of dismantling the superlab. Following his term of imprisonment, Hermosillo will be deported from the United States.

- **Bryan Galicia Barillas** (D. Mass.), aka "Chucky," a Guatemalan national who resided in Chelsea, Massachusetts, was sentenced to 22 years in prison after he pled guilty to conspiracy to conduct enterprise affairs through a pattern of racketeering activity, more commonly referred to as a RICO conspiracy. The racketeering activity by Galicia Barillas, a member of MS-13's Enfermos Criminales Salvatrucha (ECS) clique, included his involvement in the death of an innocent bystander in Chelsea. On October 18, 2014, Galicia Barillas and Hector Ramires, another member of the ECS clique, encountered a group of individuals in Chelsea suspected of belonging to a rival gang. Ramires, who was armed with a weapon that Galicia Barillas had provided on an earlier occasion, shot at one of the suspected gang rivals and missed, killing an innocent bystander who was looking out a nearby window of a room she shared with her three children. Galicia Barillas was a juvenile at the time of the murder. Galicia Barillas also accepted responsibility for his role in a September 8, 2014 stabbing and attempted murder of an individual in Chelsea, which Galicia Barillas also committed when he was a juvenile. Shortly after he turned 18, Galicia Barillas was involved in an April 2015 conspiracy to kill an MS-13 member that the gang believed was cooperating with law enforcement, and a May 26, 2015 stabbing and attempted murder of a suspected rival gang member in Chelsea. For his part, Ramires pled guilty in October 2017, to a RICO conspiracy involving murder and was sentenced in April 2018 to 27 years in prison.

- **Alfonso Rios-Ayon** (E.D. Ca.), 44, a Mexican national who resided in Pixley, California, was sentenced to 20 years in prison after he pled guilty to conspiracy to possess methamphetamine with intent to distribute it. According to court documents, between March 1, 2016 and June 29, 2016, Rios-Ayon conspired with others to distribute methamphetamine to various drug dealers and users in Kern County, California and elsewhere. On June 29, 2016, law enforcement conducted a controlled purchase of approximately 30 pounds of crystal methamphetamine at a ranch where Rios-Ayon lived. A search of the residence later resulted in the seizure of 30 pounds of crystal methamphetamine, three firearms, multiple magazines and ammunition, and approximately $16,850.

- **Felipe Benitez Aguilar** (S.D. Fla.), 44, a Mexican national who resided in West Palm Beach, Florida, was sentenced to 20 years in prison after he pled guilty to possession with intent to distribute cocaine, felon in possession of a firearm, and alien in possession of a firearm. According to court documents, Aguilar was found in possession of over 30 kilogram-sized packages of cocaine, an UZI rifle, a revolver, and multiple rounds of ammunition. Aguilar had previously been removed from the United States in February 2004, and again in July 2012. Aguilar's July 2012 removal followed his 37-month federal sentence for conspiracy to possess with intent to distribute over 500 grams of cocaine.

- **Marisol Carmona Arreola Avalos** (N.D. Tex.), a Mexican national who resided in Wilmer, Texas, was sentenced to 216 months in prison after she pled guilty to conspiracy to launder monetary instruments. According to the plea agreement, from September 25, 2015 through March 18, 2016, Marisol Avalos, and her husband, Jose Apolinar Arreola Avalos, cooked and cleaned methamphetamine in order to make the methamphetamine as white and clean as possible to maximize profits. The methamphetamine was obtained from Mexico. Marisol Avalos was provided with drug proceeds to purchase acetone, strainers, and materials to store the methamphetamine so that, once it was cleaned, it could be sold to other people in Texas and other parts of the United States. Marisol Avalos used some of the drug proceeds to pay phone bills, propane gas bills, and electric bills. The gas and electric bills were paid to maintain the house and area where the methamphetamine was cooked. The phone bill was paid so that she and Jose Avalos could communicate with other co-defendants and drug couriers who were dropping off the liquid methamphetamine to be cleaned. On March 18, 2016, the Dallas Police Department executed a search warrant at the Avalos' residence. Agents seized approximately 172 kilograms of a combination of crystal and liquid methamphetamine, firearms and several thousands of dollars.

- **Rosendo Flores Angulo** (D. N.M.), 40, a Mexican national who resided in New Mexico, was sentenced to 210 months in prison after he pled guilty to conspiracy to distribute heroin. As part of the plea agreement, Angulo admitted that he was a mid-level drug dealer who distributed heroin to low-level drug dealers and heroin users in Albuquerque in 2014 and 2015. Angulo admitted that he supplied Curtis Hutchinson, a low-level drug dealer, with heroin on April 29, 2015, and acknowledged learning that Hutchinson sold some of the heroin to a young man, who collapsed and died after using the heroin. A medical toxicologist concluded that the heroin was the cause of the young man's death. The case was initiated after Angulo was charged with heroin trafficking charges based on a number of heroin sales to two undercover DEA agents in Bernalillo and Sandoval Counties, New Mexico, between July 2015 and September 2015. Additional charges were later added which included the charge of distribution of heroin to a person who died as a result of using that heroin.

- **Ignacio Montes Leon** (W.D. Pa.), 37, a Mexican national who resided in Erie, Pennsylvania, was sentenced to 15 years in prison after he pled guilty to conspiracy to distribute between 50 to 150 kilograms of cocaine and more than 100 grams of 99% pure methamphetamine. Montes Leon was extradited from Mexico for prosecution. According to information provided to the court, Montes Leon was the local leader of a drug trafficking organization involved in importing cocaine and methamphetamine from Mexico into Texas, which was then transported to Erie, Pennsylvania and elsewhere in hidden compartments in vehicles. Montes Leon was responsible for coordinating the drug shipments with higher-level conspirators in Texas, was directly selling pure methamphetamine to individuals in Erie on multiple occasions, and was responsible for distributing multi-kilogram quantities of cocaine at a time to his co-conspirators. In December 2013, law enforcement officers seized four kilograms of cocaine in Erie, Pennsylvania connected to Montes Leon. On November 1, 2014, after Montes Leon traveled to Texas to coordinate another drug shipment, two of his drug couriers were transporting the cocaine when they were stopped by the Arkansas State Police. Montes Leon arranged for those couriers to travel to Houston, Texas area to pick up a load of cocaine destined for delivery to Erie and elsewhere. A search warrant was then executed on the vehicle and the individually-wrapped packages of cocaine were located in a hidden compartment. The packages contained more than five kilograms of cocaine. Montes Leon then fled to Mexico. Law enforcement officers located Montes Leon in Mexico, and he was arrested and extradited back to the United States to face prosecution.

- **Misraim Israel Briones Pasos**, aka Mario Ozuna (D. Ore.), 36, a Mexican national who resided in the Portland, Oregon area, was sentenced to 151 months for his role in a vast conspiracy responsible for trafficking hundreds of pounds of black tar heroin from Nayarit, Mexico to the Portland metropolitan area. According to court documents, investigators first learned of the conspiracy when a confidential informant provided a tip that co-defendant Cory Jacques was selling heroin and oxycodone from his residence in southwest Portland. Using controlled buys, surveillance, and phone records analysis, investigators determined that Jaques was receiving heroin from Briones Pasos and another co-defendant Melchor Luna Rodriguez. A federal wiretap investigation was opened in the fall of 2014. Investigators later learned that Briones Pasos managed one of several heroin cells in the Portland area sourced by a single Nayarit-based supplier. The supply cell, managed by co-defendants Christopher Guillen Robles and Paul Guillen, was responsible for bringing as much as 10 pounds of heroin into the metropolitan Portland area every week. By early 2015, investigators had revealed the cells' transportation methods and the movement of money via banks, bulk cash smuggling, and wire transfers. In February 2015, a federal grand jury in Portland returned a multi-count indictment implicating 22 defendants. Soon thereafter, investigators executed search and arrest warrants at 24 locations across four states. By February 2018, all principal targets had been convicted and the court had ordered more than $1.4 million in forfeiture money judgments. All 22 defendants have been sentenced, with sentences ranging from time-served to 151 months in prison. The 22 defendants hailed from both the United States and Mexico, with 12 being citizens of Mexico.

Immigration Status of and Pending Charges Against Known or Suspected Aliens in USMS Custody

A. Immigration Status of Known or Suspected Aliens in USMS Custody

The USMS is DOJ's component charged with the housing and care of federal pretrial detainees. USMS also houses certain short-term sentenced individuals, as well as sentenced individuals pending transfer to BOP. This report includes data on all known or suspected aliens in USMS custody.[4] As of March 31, 2018, 21,554 confirmed aliens were in USMS custody, along with 2,075 individuals for whom alienage had not yet been determined.

Confirmed aliens, identified through self-reporting or through confirmation of alienage by ICE, comprised 38 percent of the 56,436 total individuals in USMS custody. Of those confirmed aliens, 70 percent (15,065 individuals) had removal orders, 20 percent (4,383 individuals) had their immigration status currently under investigation, and approximately seven percent (1,587 individuals) were unlawfully present and in removal proceedings (*see* Figure 4). Only one percent (274 individuals) of the confirmed aliens in USMS custody were lawfully present and in immigration proceedings. Another one percent (245 individuals) of the confirmed aliens in USMS custody were in receipt of a grant of protection or relief from removal.

---

[4] USMS data reflects all aliens in USMS custody, and does not delineate solely pretrial aliens as the USMS also detains post-trial aliens completing short-term sentences or awaiting transfer to BOP.

Figure 4: Immigration Status of Confirmed Aliens in USMS Custody, FY18 Q2

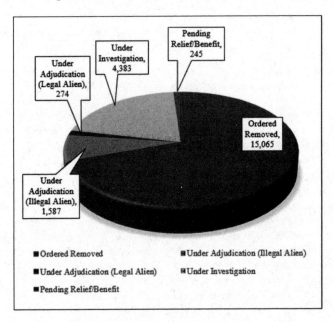

Source: U.S. Department of Justice, U.S. Department of Homeland Security

B. Pending Primary Charges Against Confirmed Aliens in USMS Custody

Of the 21,554 confirmed aliens in USMS custody, approximately 56 percent (12,121 individuals) were in custody for a primary offense related to immigration, such as human trafficking or illegal reentry after deportation (*see* Figure 5). Approximately 23 percent (4,864 individuals) of the confirmed aliens in USMS custody were in custody for a primary offense related to drugs. Other primary offenses included violations of conditions of supervision (1,062 individuals, approximately five percent of the aliens in USMS custody), property offenses (947 individuals, approximately four percent of the aliens in USMS custody), weapons offenses, and violent offenses (406 and 406 individuals, respectively, each approximately two percent of the aliens in USMS custody). Approximately four percent (955 individuals) of the aliens in USMS custody were material witnesses, while another four percent (796 individuals) were in custody for an unlisted offense or were in USMS custody due to a writ, hold, or transfer. Notably, 69 percent (14,916) of all aliens in USMS custody were apprehended in the southwest region.

Figure 5: Pending Primary Charges Against Confirmed Aliens in USMS Custody, FY18 Q2

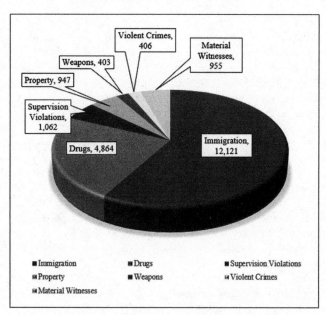

Source: U.S. Department of Justice, U.S. Department of Homeland Security

C. Costs Associated With Confirmed Aliens in USMS Custody

During the second quarter of FY18, USMS had an average daily population of 20,132 confirmed aliens in custody, and incurred more than $136 million in housing costs related to those prisoners during that quarter. An average of 3,198 of those aliens were held in BOP facilities, for whom no direct housing costs were incurred by USMS (the costs were instead funded by appropriations received by BOP). An average daily population of 82 aliens were also housed in other settings for which no direct housing costs were incurred by USMS, such as in hospitals or in correctional health care facilities due to required medical treatment. The remaining 16,853 aliens (daily average) in USMS custody were housed in a combination of state, local, and private facilities, at an average cost of $90.23 per diem.

Immigration Status of Individuals in State and Local Custody

Through its Office of Justice Programs (OJP), Bureau of Justice Statistics (BJS), DOJ continues its progress towards better understanding the immigration status of convicted aliens incarcerated in state prisons and local detention centers. In the meantime, some data is already available from particular states, such as Texas. Additionally, some information is available through public reporting of cases that offer anecdotal evidence of alien criminal activity at the state and local levels.

A. Gathering Data from State Prisons

BJS currently collects on an annual basis aggregate numbers of noncitizens in state and federal prisons through the National Prisoner Statistics program. Departments of corrections voluntarily submit these numbers. The most recent figures, released in January 2018, were from December 31, 2016. According to that report, there were approximately 83,573 inmates under federal jurisdiction or in state custody who are not U.S. citizens. As BJS appropriately noted,[5] state numbers in the report, which reflect 43,617 noncitizen individuals in custody, represent an undercount, because five states—including California, Nevada, and Oregon—did not report citizenship data. In addition, other states likely also provided undercounts, in part because; (1) inmates self-report place of birth or citizenship, and state corrections departments use these elements differently to determine citizenship, and (2) the count for most states only includes individuals in state-run institutions, not private facilities. Due to this underreporting (or complete lack of reporting) by some states, the aggregate tally of 83,573 noncitizen inmates reported to BJS as being under federal jurisdiction or in state custody does not currently represent a comprehensive national total.

BJS is improving its data collection in this area, including asking states and the BOP to provide additional information to disaggregate the number of noncitizens in custody by basic sentence length and by sex as of December 31 each year. The enhanced data collection began in January 2018, and will also include counts of noncitizens in both state-run and private facilities for all jurisdictions. BJS expects to release the 2017 counts of noncitizens soon.

BJS is also continuing its efforts to modify the National Corrections Reporting Program (NCRP), BJS's annual collection of individual-level state prisoner records, to collect citizenship status of all inmates in state prisons. In November 2018, the Office of Information and Regulatory Affairs at the Office of Management and Budget granted conditional clearance for BJS to utilize a modified NCRP.[6] The modified NCRP now also collects information regarding whether inmates in state prisons are citizens of the United States, the country of each inmate's current citizenship, and the country of each inmate's birth. BJS began data collection using the modified NCRP in early 2019.

B. Gathering Data from Local Detention Facilities

BJS currently collects data from local detention facilities through its Annual Survey of Jails (ASJ). Currently, the ASJ data cannot be used to accurately estimate the total number of

---

[5] Bureau of Justice Statistics, *Prisoners in 2016* (Jan. 2018), https://www.bjs.gov/content/pub/pdf/p16.pdf.
[6] Office of Information and Regulatory Affairs, *Notice of Office of Management and Budget Action* (Nov. 2018), https://www.reginfo.gov/public/do/DownloadNOA?requestID=292954.

noncitizens in local custody. BJS is working to improve reporting from local facilities, and develop ASJ's data collection to allow the disaggregation of conviction status, which would enable analysis of ASJ data to determine the number of noncitizens in custody, and to break those numbers down by conviction status. During the first quarter of FY18, BJS fielded a pilot study to investigate the ability of local jail facilities to report this information. Based on the results of this study, BJS is working to modify its 2019 Census of Jails (which is fielded instead of the ASJ every 5-7 years) to include this improved data collection. The 2019 Census of Jails will be fielded later this year.

In addition, the DHS, Office of Immigration Statistics is currently evaluating potential strategies to estimate the immigration status of individuals in state and local custody based on information available in the U.S. Census Bureau's American Community Survey on individuals living in institutional settings, a category that includes federal and state prisons as well as local jails.

C. Nonfederal Data and Public Reporting

While the Departments of Justice and Homeland Security are developing improved methods to collect and analyze relevant data from state and local authorities, some of those authorities already take the proactive step of making this data available to the public.

For example, the Texas Department of Public Safety publishes data online regarding criminal alien arrests and convictions. These data do not account for all aliens in the Texas criminal justice system, as they are limited to criminal alien arrestees who have had prior interaction with DHS resulting in the collection of their fingerprints. Nonetheless, these data are helpful in understanding how criminal aliens impact public safety and the criminal justice system. As reported by Texas Department of Public Safety (DPS):

> According to DHS status indicators, over 279,000 criminal aliens have been booked into local Texas jails between June 1, 2011 and January 31, 2019, of which over 189,000 were classified as illegal aliens by DHS.

> Between June 1, 2011 and January 31, 2019, these 189,000 illegal aliens were charged with more than 295,000 criminal offenses which included arrests for 539 homicide charges; 32,785 assault charges; 5,737 burglary charges; 37,234 drug charges; 403 kidnapping charges; 15,991 theft charges; 23,701 obstructing police charges; 1,660 robbery charges; 3,473 sexual assault charges; 2,170 sexual offense charges; and 2,976 weapon charges. DPS criminal history records reflect those criminal charges have thus far resulted in over 120,000 convictions including 238 homicide convictions; 13,662 assault convictions; 3,158 burglary convictions; 17,930 drug convictions; 175 kidnapping convictions; 7,100 theft convictions; 11,336 obstructing police convictions; 1,013 robbery convictions; 1,710 sexual assault convictions; 1,153 sexual offense convictions; and 1,282 weapon convictions.

These figures only count individuals who previously had an encounter with DHS that resulted in their fingerprints being entered into the DHS IDENT database. Foreign nationals who enter the country illegally and avoid detection by DHS, but are later arrested by local or state law enforcement for a state offense will not have a DHS response in regard to their lawful status and do not appear in these counts. However, in addition to the PEP [Priority Enforcement Program] program, DHS actively adjudicates the immigration status of individuals incarcerated in the Texas prison system. From 2011 to date, the Department of Criminal Justice (TDCJ) has provided DPS with information on more than 26,000 individuals who were identified by DHS as in the country illegally while they were incarcerated at TDCJ. 10,306 of these individuals were not identified through the PEP program at the time of their arrest. DPS does not know the current incarceration status of the individuals identified while they were incarcerated nor when their alien status was initially determined.[7]

D. Examples of Media Reports of Crimes Committed by Aliens at the State and Local Level

In addition to official data from state and local authorities, media reports can be helpful in understanding the impacts of aliens on public safety and the criminal justice system in the United States. Media reports are inherently less desirable than official data, in part because of the higher possibility of inaccuracies. Additionally, media reports are limited in their utility to identify larger trends, both because the reporting may be inconsistent and because media reports may be more likely to report on atypically serious crimes. Nonetheless, particularly in the absence of official data, anecdotal examples from public reporting are noted. A few examples from the second quarter of FY18 include:[8]

- **Viusqui J. Perez-Espinosa**, 45, who was convicted in Louisiana of killing his ex-girlfriend's new boyfriend, dismembering the body, and dumping the remains in a swamp. He was arrested in early 2017, several months after the murder, after severed body parts began to surface and were found by a fisherman. Perez-Espinosa is a Cuban national.[9]

---

[7] Texas Dep't of Pub. Safety, *Texas Criminal Illegal Alien Data* (last visited Feb. 15, 2019), https://www.dps.texas.gov/administration/crime_records/pages/txCriminalAlienStatistics.htm.

[8] The information contained within these examples comes entirely from the cited media reports. Neither DOJ nor DHS make any assurances as to the accuracy of the information provided in these examples, nor have DOJ or DHS independently confirmed any of the information in this section. The examples are provided solely for the purpose of demonstrating the type of information that is often contained within media reports about criminal activity.

[9] Laura McKnight, *Man convicted of killing, dismembering ex-girlfriend's new lover: Jefferson Parish DA*, The Times-Picayune (Mar. 26, 2018), https://www.nola.com/crime/index.ssf/2018/03/man_convicted_of_killing_disme.html.

- **Zheheng Feng**, 24, pled guilty to aggravated cruelty to animals after killing his girlfriend's dog and stuffing the body down a building garbage chute. Feng, a former Manhattan bank worker, was sentenced to serve 30 days in jail before being deported. He is a Chinese national.[10]

- **Abigail Hernandez**, 21, was arrested in Rochester, N.Y. in February 2018 for making threats to shoot up a high school in Rochester. Hernandez, who came to the United States illegally and was granted protection under DACA, later pled guilty.[11]

- **Ricardo Corral-Venegas**, 27, who was sentenced to 72 years to life in prison for raping one woman at knifepoint in her apartment in Aurora, Colorado, while her one-year-old son was at the apartment. Two weeks after the first rape, Corral-Venegas attempted to enter a different apartment in the same complex and sexually assault a second woman. Corral-Venegas is a former Mexican police officer from Chihuahua, Mexico, and a warrant there alleges that he raped five other women. He has entered the United States illegally at least twice, including once after being deported.[12]

Additional Information Regarding Criminal Aliens in the United States

A. Efforts to Expand the Institutional Hearing and Removal Program

The Institutional Hearing and Removal Program (IHRP) is a cooperative effort between the Executive Office for Immigration Review (EOIR), DHS, and various federal, state, and municipal corrections agencies. As part of the IHRP, DHS identifies alien inmates in BOP, state, or local custody who may be removable from the United States and initiates their removal proceedings before EOIR while the aliens continue serving their criminal sentences. Bringing immigration judges to these inmates for a determination of their removability allows their immigration case to be resolved prior to their release from incarceration. Through the IHRP, EOIR provides in-person and video teleconference immigration proceedings to determine whether alien inmates are removable from the United States and, if removable, whether they are eligible for any form of protection or relief from removal.

Upon their release from custody, DHS is able to effectuate the removal of those aliens who have a final order of removal, as determined by either an immigration judge or the Board of Immigration Appeals. IHRP aims to avoid transferring removable aliens into DHS custody, or

---

[10] Gabrielle Fonrouge, *Ex-banker gets jail, deportation for killing girlfriend's dog*, New York Post (Feb. 5, 2018), https://nypost.com/2018/02/05/ex-banker-gets-jail-deportation-for-killing-girlfriends-dog/.

[11] Frank Miles, *DACA recipient, 21, threatened to 'shoot all of ya b----es' at NY high school, police say*, Fox News (Feb. 25, 2018), https://www.foxnews.com/us/daca-recipient-21-threatened-to-shoot-all-of-ya-b-es-at-ny-high-school-police-say.

[12] Kieran Nicholson, *Former police officer from Mexico sentences to 72 years to life for sexually assaulting Aurora woman, other felonies*, The Denver Post (Mar. 21, 2018), https://www.denverpost.com/2018/03/21/ricardo-corral-venegas-sex-assault-aurora/.

releasing them into the community, pending future adjudication of their immigration case. By holding immigration proceedings during an alien's prison sentence, IHRP enhances the overall efficiency of the immigration system while contributing to the Nation's security.

Between January 1 and March 31, 2018, EOIR completed 640 immigration cases at 45 IHRP locations. EOIR had 1,963 IHRP cases pending as of March 31, 2018 and may hear cases at additional IHRP locations as circumstances warrant.

ICE ENFORCEMENT AND REMOVAL OPERATIONS REPORT

APPENDIX III

U.S. Immigration
and Customs
Enforcement

Fiscal Year 2018 ICE Enforcement
and Removal Operations Report

Overview

This report summarizes U.S. Immigration and Customs Enforcement (ICE) Enforcement and Removal Operations (ERO) activities in Fiscal Year (FY) 2018. ERO identifies, arrests, and removes aliens who present a danger to national security or a threat to public safety, or who otherwise undermine border control and the integrity of the U.S. immigration system. ICE shares responsibility for administering and enforcing the nation's immigration laws with U.S. Customs and Border Protection (CBP) and U.S. Citizenship and Immigration Services.

During FY2018, ICE ERO continued its focus on priorities laid out by two primary directives issued in 2017. On January 25, 2017, President Donald J. Trump issued Executive Order 13768, _Enhancing Public Safety in the Interior of the United States_ (EO), which set forth the Administration's immigration enforcement and removal priorities. Subsequently, the Department of Homeland Security's (DHS) February 20, 2017 implementation memorandum, _Enforcement of the Immigration Laws to Serve the National Interest_ provided further direction for the implementation of the policies set forth in the EO. Together, the EO and implementation memorandum expanded ICE's enforcement focus to include removable aliens who (1) have been convicted of any criminal offense; (2) have been charged with any criminal offense that has not been resolved; (3) have committed acts which constitute a chargeable criminal offense; (4) have engaged in fraud or willful misrepresentation in connection with any official matter before a governmental agency; (5) have abused any program related to receipt of public benefits; (6) are subject to a final order of removal but have not complied with their legal obligation to depart the United States; or (7) in the judgment of an immigration officer, otherwise pose a risk to public safety or national security. The Department continued to operate under the directive that classes or categories of removable aliens are not exempt from potential enforcement.

ICE ERO continued efforts under the direction of the 2017 EO and implementation memorandum by placing a significant emphasis on interior enforcement by protecting national security and public safety and upholding the rule of law. This report represents an analysis of ICE ERO's FY2018 year-end statistics and illustrates how ICE ERO successfully fulfilled its mission while furthering the aforementioned policies.

FY2018 Enforcement and Removal Statistics

As directed in the EO and implementation memorandum, ICE does not exempt classes or categories of removable aliens from potential enforcement. This policy directive is reflected in ERO's FY2018 enforcement statistics, which show consistent increases from previous fiscal years in the following enforcement metrics: (1) ICE ERO overall administrative arrests; (2) an accompanying rise in overall ICE removals tied to interior enforcement efforts; (3) ICE removals of criminal aliens from interior enforcement; (4) ICE removals of suspected gang members and known or suspected terrorists; (5) positive impact on ICE removals from policy initiatives including visa sanctions and diplomatic relations; (6) ICE ERO total book-ins and criminal alien book-ins; and (7) ICE ERO Detainers.

ICE ERO Administrative Arrests

An administrative arrest is the arrest of an alien for a civil violation of U.S. immigration laws, which is subsequently adjudicated by an immigration judge or through other administrative processes. With 158,581 administrative arrests in FY2018, ICE ERO recorded the greatest number of administrative arrests[1] as compared to the two previous fiscal years (depicted below in Figure 1), and the highest number since FY2014. ICE ERO made 15,111 more administrative arrests in FY2018 than in FY2017, representing an 11 percent increase, and a continued upward trend after FY2017's 30 percent increase over FY2016.

Figure 1. FY2016 – FY2018 ERO Administrative Arrests

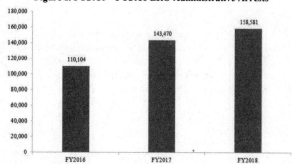

Administrative Arrests of Immigration Violators by Criminality

ICE remains committed to directing its enforcement resources to those aliens posing the greatest risk to the safety and security of the United States. By far, the largest percentage of aliens arrested by ICE are convicted criminals[2] (66 percent), followed by immigration violators with pending criminal charges[3] at the time of their arrest (21 percent). In FY2018, ERO arrested 138,117 aliens with criminal histories (convicted criminal and pending criminal charges) for an increase of 10,125 aliens over FY2017. This continued the growth seen in FY2017 when ERO arrested 26,974 more aliens with criminal histories than in FY2016 for a 27 percent gain. While the arrests of convicted criminals remained relatively level from FY 2017 to FY2018 at 105,736 and 105,140 respectively, administrative arrests with pending criminal charges increased by 48 percent. This continues the upward trend seen in FY2017, where arrests with pending charges increased by 255 percent over FY2016. Figure 2 provides a breakdown of FY2016, FY2017, and FY2018 administrative arrests by criminality.

---

[1] ERO administrative arrests include all ERO programs. All statistics are attributed to the current program of the processing officer of an enforcement action.
[2] Immigration violators with a criminal conviction entered into ICE systems of record at the time of the enforcement action.
[3] Immigration violators with pending criminal charges entered into ICE system of record at the time of the enforcement action.

Figure 2. FY2016 – FY2018 ERO Administrative Arrests by Criminality

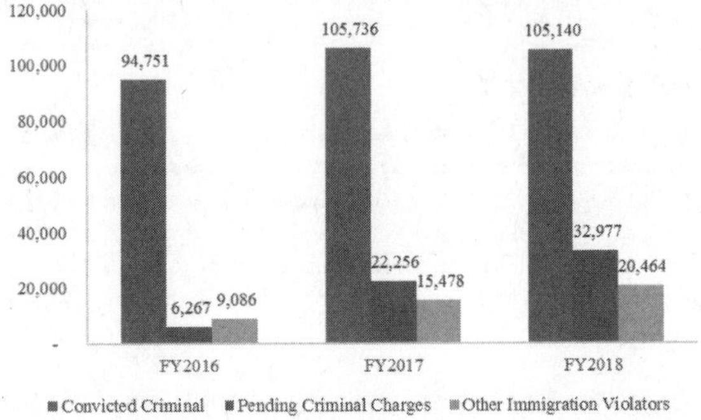

■ Convicted Criminal ■ Pending Criminal Charges ■ Other Immigration Violators

Below, Table 1 tallies all pending criminal charges and convictions by category for those aliens administratively arrested in FY2018 and lists those categories with at least 1,000 combined charges and convictions present in this population. These figures are representative of the criminal history as it is entered in the ICE system of record for individuals administratively arrested. Each administrative arrest may represent multiple criminal charges and convictions, as many of the aliens arrested by ERO are recidivist criminals.

Table 1. FY2018 Criminal Charges and Convictions for ERO Administrative Arrests

Criminal Charge Category	Criminal Charges	Criminal Convictions	Total Offenses
Traffic Offenses - DUI	26,100	54,630	80,730
Dangerous Drugs	21,476	55,109	76,585
Traffic Offenses	30,594	45,610	76,204
Immigration	11,917	51,249	63,166
Assault	20,766	29,987	50,753
Obstructing Judiciary, Congress, Legislature, Etc.	11,189	11,863	23,052
Larceny	5,295	15,045	20,340
General Crimes	8,415	10,973	19,388
Obstructing the Police	5,754	10,155	15,909
Fraudulent Activities	4,201	8,661	12,862
Burglary	2,829	9,834	12,663
Weapon Offenses	3,672	8,094	11,766
Public Peace	4,029	7,236	11,265
Invasion of Privacy	2,255	5,090	7,345
Sex Offenses (Not Involving Assault or Commercialized Sex)	1,913	4,975	6,888
Stolen Vehicle	1,693	4,568	6,261
Family Offenses	2,465	3,526	5,991
Robbery	1,139	4,423	5,562
Sexual Assault	1,610	3,740	5,350
Forgery	1,632	3,526	5,158
Damage Property	1,872	2,597	4,469
Stolen Property	1,335	3,127	4,462
Liquor	1,995	2,290	4,285
Flight / Escape	1,090	2,264	3,354
Kidnapping	791	1,294	2,085
Homicide	387	1,641	2,028
Health / Safety	522	1,242	1,764
Commercialized Sexual Offenses	729	1,010	1,739
Threat	583	791	1,374

Notes: Immigration crimes include "illegal entry," "illegal reentry," "false claim to U.S. citizenship," and "alien smuggling." "Obstructing Judiciary& Congress& Legislature& Etc.," refers to several related offenses including, but not limited to: Perjury; Contempt; Obstructing Justice; Misconduct; Parole and Probation Violations; and Failure to Appear. "General Crimes" include the following National Crime Information Center (NCIC) charges: Conspiracy, Crimes Against Person, Licensing Violation, Money Laundering, Morals - Decency Crimes, Property Crimes, Public Order Crimes, Racketeer Influenced and Corrupt Organizations Act (RICO), and Structuring.

As a result of ERO's enhanced enforcement efforts directed at restoring the integrity of the immigration system, the percentage of administrative arrests of other immigration violators[4] increased from FY2017 (11 percent) to FY2018 (13 percent). Of this population of immigration violators arrested in FY2018, Table 2 shows that 57 percent were processed with a notice to appear[5] while 23 percent were ICE fugitives[6] or subjects who had been previously removed, illegally re-entered the country (a federal felony under 8 U.S.C § 1326) and served an order of reinstatement.[7] Both the number of fugitive and illegal re-entry arrests continued a three-year trend by increasing 19 percent and 9 percent, respectively, in FY2018.

Table 2. FY2016 – FY2018 ERO Administrative Arrests of Other Immigration Violators by Arrest Type[8]

ERO Administrative Arrest Type	FY2016		FY2017		FY2018	
	Arrests	Percentage	Arrests	Percentage	Arrests	Percentage
Other Immigration Violators	9,086	100%	15,478	100%	20,464	100%
Notice to Appear	3,390	37%	7,642	49%	11,570	57%
Fugitives	1,605	18%	2,350	15%	2,791	14%
Reinstatement	758	8%	1,695	11%	1,846	9%
Other	3,333	37%	3,791	24%	4,257	21%

At-Large Arrests

An ERO at-large arrest is conducted in the community, as opposed to a custodial setting such as a prison or jail.[9] While at-large arrests remained consistent, with a 1 percent overall increase from 40,066 in FY2017 to 40,536 in FY2018 (Figure 3), at-large arrests levels remain significantly higher compared to the 30,348 from FY2016. At-large arrests of convicted criminal aliens decreased by 13 percent in FY2018 as shown in Figure 4. However, this group still constitutes the largest proportion of at-large apprehensions (57 percent). Increases year-over-year in at-large arrests of aliens with pending criminal charges (35 percent) and other immigration violators (25 percent) offset the decrease in arrests of convicted criminals. The increased enforcement of these populations without criminal convictions add to the increases seen in FY2017 for pending criminal charges (213 percent) and other immigration violators (122 percent). Again, this demonstrates ERO's commitment to removing criminal aliens and public safety threats, while still faithfully enforcing the law against all immigration violators.

---

[4] "Other Immigration Violators" are immigration violators without any known criminal convictions or pending charges entered into ICE system of record at the time of the enforcement action.
[5] A Notice to Appear (Form I-862) is the charging document that initiates removal proceedings. Charging documents inform aliens of the charges and allegations being lodged against them by ICE.
[6] A fugitive is any alien who has failed to leave the United States following the issuance of a final order of removal, deportation, or exclusion.
[7] Section 241(a)(5) of the Immigration and Nationality Act (INA) provides that DHS may reinstate (without referral to an immigration court) a final order against an alien who illegally reenters the United States after being deported, excluded, or removed from the United States under a final order.
[8] "Other" types of arrests of Other Immigration Violators include, but are not limited to, arrests for Expedited Removal, Visa Waiver Program Removal, Administrative Removal, and Voluntary Departure/Removal.
[9] ERO administrative arrests reported as "at-large" include records from all ERO Programs with Arrest Methods of Located, Non-Custodial Arrest, or Probation and Parole.

Figure 3. FY2016 – FY2018 At-Large Administrative Arrests

Figure 4. FY2016 – FY2018 At-Large Administrative Arrests by Criminality

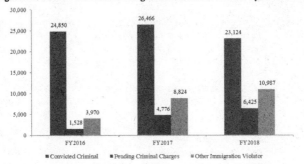

Rise in ICE Removals through enhanced Interior Enforcement

The apprehension and removal of immigration violators is central to ICE's mission to enforce U.S. immigration laws. In addition to the 11 percent increase in ERO administrative arrests from FY2017 to FY2018, ERO also made significant strides in removing aliens arrested in the interior of the country (Figure 5). Such removals stem from an ICE arrest and is the ultimate goal of the agency's interior immigration enforcement efforts. Interior ICE removals continued to increase in FY2018, as ICE removed 13,757 more aliens in this category than it did in FY2017, a 17 percent increase (Figure 5). The increases in both ERO administrative arrests and removals based on these interior arrests demonstrate the significant successes ICE achieved during FY2018, as well as the increased efficacy with which the agency carried out its mission.

Figure 5. FY2016 – FY2018 Interior ICE Removals

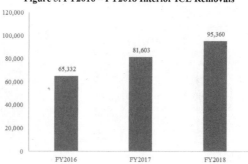

Criminal Arrests and Prosecutions

While ICE ERO showed significant gains in all meaningful enforcement metrics, perhaps none are more impressive nor have made more of an impact on public safety than its prosecutorial efforts. In conjunction with the United States Attorney's Office, ERO enforces violations of criminal immigration law through the effective prosecution of criminal offenders.

In FY2018, ERO's efforts resulted in the prosecutions of offenses which include, but are not limited to: 8 U.S.C § 1325, Illegal Entry into the United States; 8 U.S.C § 1326, Illegal Re-Entry of Removed Alien; 18 U.S.C § 1546, Fraud and Misuse of Visas, Permits and Other Documents; 18 U.S.C § 111, Assaulting and/or Resisting an Officer; and 18 U.S.C § 922(g)(5), Felon in Possession of a Firearm.

In FY2017, ERO made 5,790 criminal arrests resulting in 4,212 indictments or Bills of Information and 3,445 convictions. While these FY2017 numbers showed moderate increases over FY2016 in criminal arrests and indictments or Bills of Information, in FY2018 ERO made 7,449 criminal arrests resulting in 7,326 indictments or Bills of Information and 7,197 convictions. This surge in enforcement efforts directed at criminal aliens and repeat offenders reflects a 29 percent increase in criminal arrests, a 74 percent increase in indictments or Bills of Information, and a 109 percent increase in criminal convictions to reverse a downturn from FY2017 (Figure 6).

Figure 6. FY2016 – FY2018 Prosecution Statistics

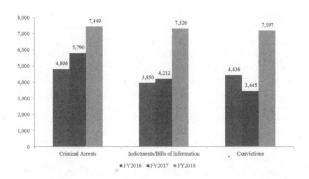

Initial Book-ins to ICE Custody

An initial book-in is the first book-in to an ICE detention facility to begin a new detention stay. This population includes aliens initially apprehended by CBP who are transferred to ICE for detention and removal. As seen in Figure 7, while overall ICE initial book-ins went down in FY2017 (323,591) compared to FY2016 (352,882), total book-ins increased in FY2018 to 396,448, illustrating the ongoing surge in illegal border crossings.

Figure 7 shows the number of book-ins resulting from ICE and CBP enforcement efforts for FY2016, FY2017, and FY2018.[10] Notably, book-ins from CBP increased 32 percent in FY2018 to 242,778, while book-ins from ICE arrests continued an upward trend from FY2017's 29 percent increase with an additional increase of 10 percent in FY2018.

Figure 7. FY2016 – FY2018 Initial Book-ins to ICE Detention by Arresting Agency

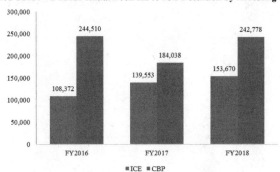

---

[10] CBP enforcement efforts represent records that were processed by Border Patrol, Inspections, Inspections-Air, Inspections-Land, and Inspections-Sea.

Detainers

A detainer is a request to the receiving law enforcement agency to both notify DHS as early as practicable before a removable alien is released from criminal custody, and to maintain custody of the alien for a period not to exceed 48 hours beyond the time the alien would otherwise have been released to allow DHS to assume custody for removal purposes. ICE issues detainers to federal, state, and local law enforcement agencies only after establishing probable cause that the subject is an alien who is removable from the United States and to provide notice of ICE's intent to assume custody of a subject detained in that law enforcement agency's custody. The detainer facilitates the custodial transfer of an alien to ICE from another law enforcement agency. This process may reduce potential risks to ICE officers and to the general public by allowing arrests to be made in a controlled, custodial setting as opposed to at-large arrests in the community.

The cooperation ICE receives from other law enforcement agencies is critical to its ability to identify and arrest aliens who pose a risk to public safety or national security. Some jurisdictions do not cooperate with ICE as a matter of state or local law, executive order, judicial rulings, or policy. All detainers issued by ICE are accompanied by either: (1) a properly completed Form I-200 (Warrant for Arrest of Alien) signed by a legally authorized immigration officer; or (2) a properly completed Form I-205 (Warrant of Removal/Deportation) signed by a legally authorized immigration officer, both of which include a determination of probable cause of removability.

Issued Detainers
In FY2018, ERO issued 177,147 detainers – an increase of 24 percent from the 142,356 detainers issued in FY2017 (Figure 8). This number demonstrates the large volume of illegal aliens involved in criminal activity and the public safety risk posed by these aliens, as well as ERO's commitment to taking enforcement action against all illegal aliens it encounters. The rise in detainers issued continues the trend from FY2017's 65 percent growth over FY2016 and shows a consistent focus on interior enforcement, particularly for those aliens involved in criminal activity, despite continued opposition and lack of cooperation from uncooperative jurisdictions.

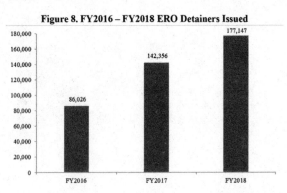

Figure 8. FY2016 – FY2018 ERO Detainers Issued

ICE Removals

Integral to the integrity of the nation's lawful immigration system is the removal of immigration violators who are illegally present in the country and have received a final order of removal.[11] A removal is defined as the compulsory and confirmed movement of an inadmissible or deportable alien out of the United States based on such an order.[12] ICE removals include both aliens arrested by ICE and aliens who were apprehended by CBP and turned over to ICE for repatriation efforts. In FY2018, ICE saw a significant increase in both overall removals as well as removals where ICE was the initial arresting agency.

Figure 9 displays total ICE removals for FY2016, FY2017, and FY2018 and highlights the 13 percent increase from 226,119 to 256,085 in FY2018. After a drop in FY2017 overall removals stemming from historic lows in border crossings, ICE removals rebounded in FY2018, with the previously identified 17 percent increase stemming from both strengthened ICE interior enforcement efforts as well as an 11 percent increase in removals of border apprehensions.

Figure 10 breaks down ICE removals by arresting agency, which demonstrates a 46 percent increase from FY2016 to FY2018 (from 65,332 to 95,360) in removals tied to ICE arrests.

Figure 9. FY2016 – FY2018 ICE Removals

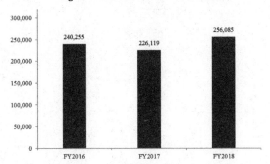

---

[11] ICE removals include removals and returns where aliens were turned over to ICE for removal efforts. This includes aliens processed for Expedited Removal (ER) or Voluntary Return (VR) that are turned over to ICE for detention. Aliens processed for ER and not detained by ERO or VRs after June 1st, 2013 and not detained by ICE are primarily processed by the U.S. Border Patrol. CBP should be contacted for those statistics.
[12] Ibid.

Figure 10. FY2016 – FY2018 ICE Removals by Arresting Agency

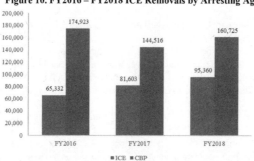

Figure 11 shows the breakdown of ICE removals based on criminal history. ICE removals of convicted criminals followed overall removal trends with a small decrease from 138,669 in FY2016 to 127,699 in FY2017, while rising to 145,262 in FY2018, a 14 percent increase. Over this same period, ICE removals of aliens with pending criminal charges has steadily increased from 12,163 in FY2016 to 16,374 in FY2017 for a 35 percent increase and to 22,796 in FY2018 for another 39 percent increase over the previous year.

Figure 11. FY2016 – FY2018 ICE Removals by Criminality

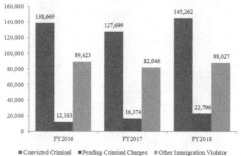

ICE Removals to Ensure National Security and Public Safety

ICE removals of known or suspected gang members and known or suspected terrorists (KST) are instrumental to ICE's national security and public safety missions, and the agency directs significant resources to identify, locate, arrest, and remove these aliens.

ICE identifies gang members and KSTs by checking an alien's background in federal law enforcement databases, interviews with the aliens, and information received from law enforcement partners. This information is flagged accordingly in ICE's enforcement systems. These populations are not mutually exclusive, as an alien may be flagged as both a known or suspected gang member, and a KST. As seen in Figure 12, ICE removals of known and suspected gang members increased by 162 percent in FY2017, more than doubling from the previous year. These critical removals increased again in FY2018, rising by 9 percent from FY2017. ICE's KST removals also rose significantly between FY2016 and FY2017 (Figure 13), increasing by 67 percent, while removals of aliens in this group were relatively level in FY2018, with ICE conducting 42 removals compared to 45 in FY2017.

Figure 12. FY2016 – FY2018 ICE Removals of Known or Suspected Gang Members

Figure 13. FY2016 – FY2018 ICE Removals of Known or Suspected Terrorists

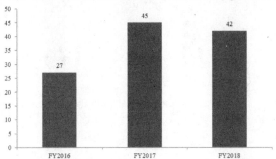

Removals of USBP Family Unit and Unaccompanied Alien Children Apprehensions

Since the initial surge at the Southwest border SWB) in FY2014, there has been a significant increase in the arrival of both family units (FMUAs) and unaccompanied alien children (UACs). In FY2018, approximately 50,000 UACs and 107,000 aliens processed as FMUAs were apprehended at the SWB by the U.S. Border Patrol (USBP). These numbers represent a marked increase from FY2017, when approximately 41,000 UACs and 75,000 FMUA were apprehended by USBP. While USBP routinely turns FMUA apprehensions over to ICE for removal proceedings, ICE is severely limited by various laws and judicial actions from detaining family units through the completion of removal proceedings. For UAC apprehensions, DHS is responsible for the transfer of custody to the Department of Health and Human Services (HHS) within 72 hours, absent exceptional circumstances. HHS is similarly limited in their ability to detain UACs through the pendency of their removal proceedings. When these UACs are released by

HHS, or FMUA are released from DHS custody, they are placed onto the non-detained docket, which currently has more than 2,641,589 cases and results in decisions not being rendered for many years. Further, even when removal orders are issued, very few aliens from the non-detained docket comply with these orders and instead join an ever-growing list of 565,892 fugitive aliens.

In FY2018, ICE removed 2,711 aliens identified as FMUAs from USBP apprehension data. As seen in Figure 14, this number is up from 2,326 removals of FMUAs in FY2017, resulting in a 17 percent increase. This maintains the upward trend from FY2017, where ICE removals of this population increased by 35 percent over FY2016 (1,728). ICE similarly identifies UACs based on USBP apprehensions, and in FY2018 ICE removed 5,571 UACs, a 55 percent increase over the 3,598 UACs removed in FY2017 (Figure 15). FY2017 similarly showed an increase in UAC removals when ICE removed 41 percent more UACs compared to FY2016's 2,545. Most of the remaining population of UAC and FMUA who have been apprehended, remain in the country awaiting completion of their removal proceedings or defying removal orders.

Figure 14. FY2016 – FY2018 ICE Removals of USBP-Identified Family Unit Apprehensions

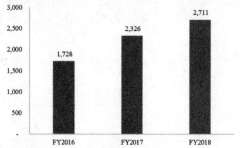

Figure 15. FY2016 – FY2018 ICE Removals of USBP-Identified UAC Apprehensions

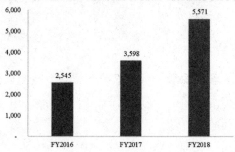

Effects of Visa Sanctions and Diplomatic Relations

On September 13, 2017, DHS announced the implementation of visa sanctions[13] on Cambodia, Eritrea, Guinea, and Sierra Leone due to a lack of historical cooperation from these countries with regard to accepting their nationals who have been ordered removed. In coordination with the U.S. Department of State (DoS), consular officers in these countries were ordered to implement visa restrictions on specific categories of visa applicants. The categories were determined on a country-by-country basis. If the impacted countries did not respond appropriately, the scope of the sanctions could be expanded to include more visa applicant categories. The result of these sanctions can be seen in the ICE removals statistics for these countries in Table 3. All the countries with newly-issued visa sanctions have greater removals in FY2018 than in FY2017. In addition to visa sanctions, DHS and DoS have coordinated to improve diplomatic relations with Cuba, resulting in a 189 percent increase of Cuban national removals from FY2017 to FY2018. ICE continues to work with DHS and DoS to invoke visa sanctions where appropriate for the purpose of fostering better cooperation with foreign countries in the context of removals.

Table 3. FY2017 – FY2018 ICE Removals from Visa Sanction Countries and Cuba

Country of Citizenship	FY2017	FY2018	% Change
CAMBODIA	29	110	279%
CUBA	160	463	189%
ERITREA	41	62	51%
GUINEA	88	219	149%
SIERRA LEONE	44	79	80%
Total	**362**	**933**	**158%**

Conclusion

As the agency primarily responsible for immigration enforcement efforts in the interior of the United States, ICE plays a critical role in fulfilling the requirements laid out in The President's EO and DHS' subsequent implementation memorandum. The statistics in this report illustrate ICE's commitment to these policies and success in implementing them during FY2018.

ICE ERO's FY2018 statistics demonstrate the agency's strengthened interior enforcement measures and show significant success in identifying, arresting, and removing aliens who are in violation of U.S. law, particularly those who pose a public safety or national security threat. This was accomplished despite limited resources and an increasingly challenging operational environment.

In FY2018, ICE ERO conducted 158,581 overall administrative arrests, 15,111 more than in FY2017, while it conducted 256,085 removals – the highest level since FY2014, resulting in a more than 10 percent increase in overall arrests and removals. ICE continues to prioritize its limited resources on public safety threats and immigration violators, as reflected by the fact that, like in FY2017, 9 out of 10 ERO administrative arrests had either a criminal conviction(s), pending charge(s), were an ICE fugitive, or illegally reentered the country after previously being removed. These results clearly demonstrate that the increased enforcement productivity in FY2017 has maintained an upward trend, and that ICE's efforts to

---

[13] Section 243(d) of the INA states that, upon notification from the Secretary of Homeland Security, the Secretary of State shall direct consular officers to stop issuing visas to immigrants, nonimmigrants, or both, from countries that unreasonably delay or fail entirely to repatriate their nationals.

restore integrity to our nation's immigration system and enhance the safety and security of the United States have continued to yield positive results.

Appendix A: Methodology

Data Source:
Data used to report ICE statistics are obtained through the ICE Integrated Decision Support (IIDS) system data warehouse.

Data Run Dates:
FY2018: IIDS v.1.34 run date 10/08/2018; ENFORCE Integrated Database (EID) as of 10/06/2018
FY2017: IIDS v.1.28 run date 10/09/2017; ENFORCE Integrated Database (EID) as of 10/07/2017
FY2016: IIDS v.1.22.1 run date 10/04/2016; ENFORCE Integrated Database (EID) as of 10/02/2016

Removals
ICE Removals include removals and returns initiated by ICE and those initiated by other agencies in which aliens were turned over to ICE for repatriation efforts. Returns include Voluntary Returns, Voluntary Departures, and Withdrawals Under Docket Control. Any voluntary return recorded on or after June 1, 2013 without an ICE intake case is not recorded as an ICE removal.

Removals data are historical and remain static. In FY2009, ICE began to "lock" removal statistics on October 5 at the end of each fiscal year, and counted only aliens whose removal or return was already confirmed. Aliens removed or returned in that fiscal year but not confirmed until after October 5 were excluded from the locked data, and thus from ICE statistics. To ensure an accurate and complete representation of all removals and returns, ICE will count removals and returns confirmed after October 5 toward the next fiscal year. FY2016 removals, excluding FY2015 "lag," were 235,524. The number of removals in FY2017, excluding the "lag" from FY2016, was 220,649. The number of removals in FY2018, excluding the "lag" from FY2017, was 252,405.

Appendix B: FY2017 and FY2018 Removals by Country of Citizenship[14]

FY2017 and FY2018 ICE Removals by Country of Citizenship		
Country of Citizenship	FY2017	FY2018
MEXICO	128,765	141,045
GUATEMALA	33,570	50,390
HONDURAS	22,381	28,894
EL SALVADOR	18,838	15,445
DOMINICAN REPUBLIC	1,986	1,769
BRAZIL	1,413	1,691
ECUADOR	1,152	1,264
COLOMBIA	1,082	1,162
HAITI	5,578	934
NICARAGUA	832	879
JAMAICA	782	792
CHINA, PEOPLES REPUBLIC OF	525	726
INDIA	460	611
PERU	458	581
CUBA	160	463
ROMANIA	292	403
NIGERIA	312	369
CANADA	353	342
VENEZUELA	248	336
GHANA	305	243
PAKISTAN	177	235
SOMALIA	521	229
GUINEA	88	219
PHILIPPINES	182	217
SPAIN	172	209
UNITED KINGDOM	151	209
CHILE	129	166
COSTA RICA	151	162
BANGLADESH	203	147
GUYANA	137	142
KENYA	103	140
SAUDI ARABIA	139	135
ITALY	117	125
SENEGAL	197	125

---

[14] Country of citizenship is reported as it appears in ICE's system of record at the time data is pulled but may be updated as additional information is discovered or verified.

FY2017 and FY2018 ICE Removals by Country of Citizenship		
Country of Citizenship	FY2017	FY2018
POLAND	120	123
SOUTH KOREA	113	122
VIETNAM	71	122
ARGENTINA	102	121
LIBERIA	107	113
GAMBIA	56	111
CAMBODIA	29	110
INDONESIA	68	110
RUSSIA	127	107
UKRAINE	86	105
TRINIDAD AND TOBAGO	128	104
BAHAMAS	95	101
MICRONESIA, FEDERATED STATES OF	110	99
ALBANIA	55	98
MAURITANIA	8	98
PORTUGAL	65	96
JORDAN	98	94
ISRAEL	81	93
BELIZE	82	91
EGYPT	57	85
FRANCE	82	85
TURKEY	93	85
IVORY COAST	13	82
BOLIVIA	76	81
HUNGARY	116	81
DEM REP OF THE CONGO	34	79
SIERRA LEONE	44	79
CAMEROON	58	72
GERMANY	75	72
CAPE VERDE	29	68
MALI	34	63
ERITREA	41	62
SOUTH SUDAN	2	61
PANAMA	69	59
MOROCCO	67	58
THAILAND	33	55
LEBANON	35	51
LITHUANIA	26	49

FY2017 and FY2018 ICE Removals by Country of Citizenship		
Country of Citizenship	FY2017	FY2018
IRAQ	61	48
BOSNIA-HERZEGOVINA	47	47
CZECH REPUBLIC	30	47
IRELAND	34	47
URUGUAY	38	47
NEPAL	45	45
SOUTH AFRICA	23	42
SUDAN	19	42
UNKNOWN	26	42
UZBEKISTAN	28	41
BURMA	10	40
NETHERLANDS	40	40
AUSTRALIA	22	39
MOLDOVA	34	38
ETHIOPIA	46	36
SRI LANKA	41	36
BURKINA FASO	31	35
MARSHALL ISLANDS	22	35
SLOVAKIA	20	35
BULGARIA	26	34
ANGOLA	7	32
KOREA	44	32
AFGHANISTAN	48	30
KAZAKHSTAN	14	30
SAMOA	13	30
SERBIA	18	30
JAPAN	13	28
MONGOLIA	23	28
ST. LUCIA	23	28
ARMENIA	24	27
TAIWAN	28	27
ANTIGUA-BARBUDA	19	24
NEW ZEALAND	16	24
TOGO	19	24
YEMEN	10	24
GREECE	20	22
IRAN	22	22
FIJI	13	21

FY2017 and FY2018 ICE Removals by Country of Citizenship		
Country of Citizenship	FY2017	FY2018
TONGA	13	21
GEORGIA	22	20
DOMINICA	10	19
SURINAME	7	19
SWEDEN	19	19
TANZANIA	13	19
ZIMBABWE	12	19
CONGO	5	18
MACEDONIA	10	18
MONTENEGRO	9	18
ALGERIA	28	17
BARBADOS	19	17
BELGIUM	9	17
LATVIA	19	17
TUNISIA	7	16
HONG KONG	9	15
KYRGYZSTAN	17	15
ST. KITTS-NEVIS	16	15
AZERBAIJAN	8	14
BURUNDI	6	14
KOSOVO	10	14
CHAD	7	13
ESTONIA	12	13
ST. VINCENT-GRENADINES	10	13
UGANDA	11	13
CROATIA	5	12
ZAMBIA	10	12
KUWAIT	12	11
MALAYSIA	8	11
BELARUS	10	10
BENIN	8	10
GRENADA	15	9
PALAU	15	9
LAOS	5	8
LIBYA	9	8
TAJIKISTAN	9	8
AUSTRIA	7	7
NORWAY	4	7

FY2017 and FY2018 ICE Removals by Country of Citizenship		
Country of Citizenship	FY2017	FY2018
SYRIA	2	7
GABON	3	6
PARAGUAY	5	6
SINGAPORE	4	6
BERMUDA	3	5
EQUATORIAL GUINEA	2	5
GUINEA-BISSAU	4	5
NIGER	20	5
YUGOSLAVIA	4	5
CZECHOSLOVAKIA	6	4
SWITZERLAND	5	4
TURKS AND CAICOS ISLANDS	4	4
CYPRUS	1	3
DJIBOUTI	1	3
FINLAND	3	3
MALAWI	4	3
CENTRAL AFRICAN REPUBLIC	1	2
DENMARK	5	2
ICELAND	1	2
NAMIBIA	1	2
NETHERLANDS ANTILLES	2	2
QATAR	4	2
RWANDA	10	2
SERBIA AND MONTENEGRO	2	2
TURKMENISTAN	9	2
UNITED ARAB EMIRATES	3	2
ARUBA	1	1
BAHRAIN	1	1
BHUTAN	0	1
BOTSWANA	3	1
BRITISH VIRGIN ISLANDS	3	1
GUADELOUPE	0	1
LESOTHO	0	1
MACAU	0	1
MADAGASCAR	1	1
MALDIVES	0	1
MONTSERRAT	0	1
PAPUA NEW GUINEA	1	1

FY2017 and FY2018 ICE Removals by Country of Citizenship		
Country of Citizenship	FY2017	FY2018
SLOVENIA	1	1
ANDORRA	1	0
CAYMAN ISLANDS	2	0
FRENCH GUIANA	1	0
LUXEMBOURG	1	0
MAURITIUS	1	0
MOZAMBIQUE	2	0
OMAN	3	0
SAN MARINO	1	0
SWAZILAND	1	0
Total	226,119	256,085

LETTER OF COMMENDATION FROM GENERAL PEDE FOR CAPTAIN PINSKER'S OUTSTANDING PERFORMANCE

February 25, 2019

Captain Matt Pinsker

████████████████
████████████████

Dear Captain Pinsker:

MG Risch and I would like to commend you for your outstanding performance while detailed as a federal prosecutor with the US Attorney's Office. Your contributions directly led to the successful completion of this important mission. We appreciate the personal sacrifices required by you and your family as you spent months away from home. You and your fellow Judge Advocates exemplified the great expertise and dedication to excellence that form the bedrock of our Corps. We are proud of you.

As a Corps, we must remain ready for the current conflicts and those yet to come. Your ability to answer the call upon short notice is emblematic of that readiness and exemplifies the posture we must maintain as a force. Stay ready, stay focused and keep up the great work.

Be Ready!

Charles N. Pede
Lieutenant General, USA
The Judge Advocate General

Stuart W. Risch
Major General, USA
Deputy Judge Advocate General

TEXT OF PLAQUE AWARDED TO CAPTAIN PINSKER FOR HIS SERVICE ON THE BORDER

United States Attorney's Office
Southern District of Texas

In appreciation of exceptional service to the mission of the United States Department of Justice and the United States Attorney's Office, Southern District of Texas.

CAPT Matt Clay Pinsker
2018

INDEX